To A Great
Teacher

Earl W Carter
June 2018

AN EAST TEXAS FAMILY'S CIVIL WAR

LIBRARY OF SOUTHERN CIVILIZATION

AN EAST TEXAS FAMILY'S CIVIL WAR

THE LETTERS OF NANCY & WILLIAM WHATLEY, MAY–DECEMBER 1862

Edited by **JOHN T. WHATLEY**
Foreword by **Jacqueline Jones**

LOUISIANA STATE UNIVERSITY PRESS   BATON ROUGE

Published by Louisiana State University Press
Copyright © 2019 by Louisiana State University Press
All rights reserved
Manufactured in the United States of America
First printing

Designer: Barbara Neely Bourgoyne
Typeface: Ingeborg
Printer and binder: Sheridan Books

The William J. Whatley Letters are reproduced here with the permission of the Dolph
Briscoe Center for American History at the University of Texas, Austin.

Cataloging-in-Publication Data are available from the Library of Congress.
ISBN 978-0-8071-7069-4 (cloth: alk. paper) — ISBN 978-0-8071-7131-8 (pdf) —
ISBN 978-0-8071-7132-5 (epub)

The paper in this book meets the guidelines for permanence and durability of the
Committee on Production Guidelines for Book Longevity of the Council on Library
Resources. ♾

For Melba

I am sick and tired of trying to do a man's business when I am nothing more than a contemptible poor piece of multiplying human flesh tied to the house by a crying young one, looked upon as belonging to a race of inferior beings.

LIZZIE NEBLETT, Texas housewife and letter writer, Anderson, Texas, 1862

Let me tell you what is coming. After the sacrifice of countless millions of treasure and hundreds of thousands of lives you may win Southern independence, but I doubt it. The North is determined to preserve this Union. They are not a fiery, impulsive people as you are, for they live in colder climates. But when they begin to move in a given direction, they move with the steady momentum and perseverance of a mighty avalanche.

SAM HOUSTON, Galveston speech, April 19, 1861

CONTENTS

MAPS

FOREWORD

The wartime correspondence between William Jefferson Whatley and Nancy Falkaday Whatley, husband and wife, spans only half the year of 1862. Yet here in these letters, written between May 23 and December 31, are found in compressed form many of the grand, sweeping themes that marked the Civil War, which lasted for four long, bloody years. In just a seven-month period, the Whatleys suffered the devastating effects of the war, on the home front and in Confederate military encampments. Their initial optimism—that the war would be short, that they could keep intact their small plantation—gradually gave way to despair. Their letters chronicle the dislocations caused by troop mobilization and the grinding, everyday slog of a conflagration that would seem to go on forever among those engulfed by it.

The Whatleys' correspondence tells the moving story of a young couple and their four children, with Nancy (age twenty-five) remaining at home in the vicinity of Caledonia, Rusk County, Texas, and William (age thirty-one) deployed to Arkansas. The couple were separated by a relatively short distance—Nancy, in northeast Texas near the Louisiana line, was about three hundred miles from William when he was stationed at Camp Nelson in central Arkansas. Nevertheless, to them the distance felt vast, and they relied on writing and receiving letters to maintain contact with each other. When William left for the front, Nancy assumed charge of the small plantation, which depended on thirteen enslaved workers to tend cows, chickens, pigs, horses, and a mule; grow corn, peas, potatoes, turnips, and cotton; and produce cotton cloth. The Whatleys' letters to each other reveal the difficulties she faced overseeing enslaved workers, and the deprivations and frustrations he endured on the march and in camp. Their affection for each other and for their children is palpable, their attention to the details of everyday life illuminating.

At the same time, as a historical source and a particular literary genre, the letters pose three main challenges for the reader. The first concerns the motivation of the correspondents themselves. Did husband and wife each try to minimize the hardships they faced in order to put the other's mind at ease? For example, William boasts that he is enjoying robust health and is gaining weight in camp: Can the reader accept his claims at face value? Or is he consciously trying to reassure his anxious, harried wife? In any case, both seem to be keeping up a brave front for the other, suggesting we need to be cautious in assessing their state of mind as well as their material circumstances while writing the letters.

The second concerns the behavior of William and Nancy's neighbor, Mr. Martin, who has agreed to help Nancy manage the day-to-day operations in her husband's absence. Both William and Nancy express keen disappointment, if not anger, when Martin does not live up to their expectations. Seen from the Whatleys' perspective, Martin appears irresponsible and unfeeling, as the young wife makes seemingly heroic efforts to keep the place and her family together in William's absence. Yet it is possible that Martin had his own household to worry about—perhaps ill children, sons away at war and wounded or even recently killed, or obligations imposed upon him by extended kin. We know that he proves to be an unreliable friend to the Whatleys, but we do not know the reasons for his inconstancy. Nancy seems resentful when he complains that her hogs have trampled his cornfield, but perhaps his trials were just as heavy as—or heavier than—hers. Did he callously betray the couple, or did he do his best under harrowing conditions?

Finally, we must glean from Nancy's writings—an inadequate source to be sure, but the only one available—hints about the struggles of the Whatleys' enslaved workers during these months in 1862. The six adults and six or seven children too endured the wrenching effects of war. We get glimpses of the liberties they took, the opportunities they seized, once William was away from home and Nancy found herself consumed by her roles as housekeeper, mother, and plantation manager. After the cotton crop was laid by (i.e., planted) in early June, these workers seemed impervious to her entreaties to toil hard at other tasks around the place. They shirked work and gave a neighboring white man "some saucy jaw." When they claimed to be unwell and unable to labor in the fields, were they feigning illness or not? That they remained on the property suggests they made a shrewd calculation—that as individuals and family members they would be better off in a familiar place, one that provided them with sufficient food and shelter. If they fled and took their chances on the open road, they would be vulnerable to bushwhackers, Confederate soldiers, and citizen patrols. It is therefore incumbent on the reader to keep in mind that the Whatleys' aim to keep the small plantation functioning according to prewar routines was not the aim of their enslaved workers, who began to test the limits of bondage as soon as William left home.

William spoke for many of his comrades-in-arms early in the war when he proclaimed that he was "battling" for Nancy against advancing Union forces. He could at times fall back on his own bravado to reassure his wife that he would protect his family, telling her that "we are a perfect terror to the feds," and assuring the children he would return home soon, but only after he "kill[ed] all the Yankees." William believed that white Southerners should forge their own nation; at the same time, he exhibited a great deal of pride as a Texan. In May of 1862 he could hardly foresee the ways that his commitment to military service would lead to the disruption—and in some respects the destruction—of the ideas and people he held dear.

Indeed, the short life of the would-be new nation was riddled with ironies and contradictions. William left home to defend his family, yet his wife and children endured intense hardship and remained vulnerable to disease and physical privation throughout his absence. He left home to fulfill his obligations as a father and a husband, and yet his absence upended gender roles and forced Nancy to assume the responsibilities of both husband and wife, father and mother, overseer and housekeeper, disciplinarian and nurturer. Nancy fretted about fencing for the fields, the lack of rain, the whereabouts of her livestock, a broken well, and the price their crops would fetch on the market. Meanwhile, William was learning to cook and do the laundry.

William fought to preserve the institution of slavery, yet the heart of that institution was plantation discipline, which began to unravel as soon as he mounted his horse to join his regiment. Contending with long, forced marches, wet and muddy conditions, primitive shelter, uncertain food supplies, and homesickness, William complains at one point that his slaves are "having a much easier time than their master." He resents the fact that they are able to remain with their families amid the familiar routines of the growing season, while he endures long stretches of boredom and uncertainty about the immediate future. At one point he compares the soldiers' winter quarters to slave cabins.

Like many other planters and farmers, William recognizes that wartime conditions have put the lie to antebellum ideologies about the nature of slavery and the enslaved. According to these ideas— and myths—slaves were childlike creatures, unable to act without white supervision and grateful for the so-called "security" that bondage afforded them. In her first letters, Nancy notes with relief that the enslaved men are proving to be obedient. Yet it soon becomes clear that Marshall, Sam, and the others cannot be trusted to follow long-established patterns of plantation maintenance and field work. They labor indifferently, or not at all. William fears that the place will go "to rack" because of their negligence. Hence his conviction that Mr. Martin must help Nancy to keep order and use force if necessary to make the slaves work. Wartime exigencies unmasked the prewar shibboleth of white-black harmony—"my family black and white," a favorite saying among slave owners. That notion now gave way to angry recriminations against "unfaithful" slaves, with William threatening to sell the workers who so boldly defied his wife. When Marshall speaks disrespectfully to a Mr. Miller, the white man says he will have to show him that "white is white," implying that either physical force against the black man or sale away from his family is the only sure remedy for such reckless, defiant behavior on the part of a slave.

In the late spring of 1862, both William and Nancy express hopefulness about the eventual outcome of the conflict and their ability to weather it. William expects that peace will arrive within the year, and with it the independence of the Confederate nation. Nancy is determined to keep the place going, and she demonstrates a keen understanding of all aspects of plantation management, even as she acknowledges that she has her hands very full. Soon, though, the harsh realities of war intrude for both husband and wife, and their initial optimism recedes in the wake of resentment and finger pointing toward Mr. Martin and their enslaved workers. Again, their shifting perspectives mirror those of other Southern white men and women, as the conflict began to take its horrific toll in both material and emotional ways.

Like many Confederate soldiers, William expects that his skill with guns and horses will lead to a brief, glorious romp over the city-bred, weak-kneed Yankees. Initially he embraces camp life as an opportunity for fellowship among like-minded men and extended kinfolk. Soon, however, he has to deal with the fact that there is not enough forage to make a cavalry regiment viable. He notes with disapproval the presence of "profane," hard-drinking men in camp, the high prices for everything, and the critical shortages of notepaper. Instead of dispatching Union forces from horseback, he spends most of his time on the march, wading through water and sleeping on the wet, muddy ground. He must also perform fatigue work, which includes such duties as digging latrines and building fortifications—work fit for slaves but not white men. Though he is able to avoid the dire fate of many of his friends, kin, and comrades—men who suffer from illness or become wounded and then die—he is bored and miserable while waiting for deployment. As the casualties mount, he begins to question the meaning of the war and the nature of Confederate leaders, condemning (by early November) "this wicked and unnatural war." His frustration with army life reveals not only his own physical discomfort, but also his increasing fears about Nancy's plight back home.

At the beginning of the conflict, Nancy assumes that past farming practices will still pertain and that through sheer force of will she will prevail in overseeing the enslaved labor force that will harvest and market their crops. Yet circumstances gradually overwhelm her. A severe drought threatens the whole enterprise, her children become ill, and "the negroes will not work." She contemplates selling some of the enslaved workers, or hiring them out to another landowner. However, the influx of a large number of slaves into the state made those possibilities unlikely. Many plantation owners from the Mississippi Valley and even beyond hoped to "refugee" their enslaved labor forces—that is, get them out of the way of both Union forces and Confederate press agents, military officials who might seize them for fatigue work. Given an oversupply of slaves in Texas, then, Nancy's options for ridding herself of her slaves and profiting in the process were limited. The declining value of Confederate money made financial transactions of any kind problematic in any case.

Both Whatleys are aware that support for the Confederacy among white Southerners is not universal and that what support existed in the spring of 1861 began to erode among certain groups not long after. They have contempt for deserters, but at the same time they appreciate the hardship visited upon white families when husbands, fathers, sons, and brothers are conscripted into the army. In fact, they both hope that Mr. Martin will be able to avoid the draft so that he can help Nancy manage the small plantation. Yet overall, deserters proved to be a destructive and unpredictable lot. In his last letter of December 31, William writes that the countryside is "running wild" with them. Called variously "Jayhawkers" and "bushwhackers," they have become armed bandits, plundering homesteads, tormenting slaves, and generally wreaking havoc on the civilian population.

Nancy and William remain separated by miles and by the everyday worlds in which they live—she preoccupied by crops and livestock, caring for their children, and the recalcitrance of their slaves; he enduring camp life and worrying about where he can buy a few pieces of notepaper. At the same time, the very real threat of ubiquitous epidemics, and especially the deadly scourge of measles, unites them. The letters provide insight into how and why microbes took such a devastating toll on soldiers and civilians, enslaved and free, alike. The wartime Southern population was constantly churning, with soldiers coming home for furlough and then returning to the front, whole households relocating or seeking refuge, and large numbers of enslaved workers facing impressment by Confederate authorities. In military camps, soldiers lived in close quarters, their resistance lowered by poor food and inadequate shelter. They succumbed in large numbers to disease.

The letters written by both Nancy and William provide a chronicle of loved ones, comrades-in-arms, enslaved people, and anonymous victims swept away by the measles. From the very beginning, William is sensitive to the awful effects of this disease in camp, effects that knew no distinctions of class, rank, skin color, or legal status. Meanwhile, in early June, Nancy has to contend with measles in her own household, when two of the enslaved children contract the disease. This reality, plus Nancy's belief that the disease was "brought in by the soldiers," means that she is constantly anxious about what will happen if she herself falls ill, and constantly aware of the potential danger for her own family. "I am in daily dread," she writes at one point. These worries arise as she faces new and urgent challenges—to sell the property back to a Mr. Jones, from whom they had originally bought the land, in order to escape the debt they owe her father; and then to make arrangements so that the residents of the place, enslaved and free, can be moved to her parents' home not far away. Her father begins to devise contingency plans; if Nancy becomes ill, he and her mother will care for her. William assures her that if she is afflicted, it will be only a mild case, and that the proper cure will be to avoid any kind of medicinal remedies.

An estimated 700,000 combatants died during the Civil War—more Americans than in all other U.S. military conflicts (since the Revolution and through the wars in Iraq and Afghanistan) combined. Historians have described in great detail the carnage on the battlefield, but increasingly they have also focused on the drama that unfolded on the home front, where white women boldly stepped out of their "sphere" to take over the work of their planter-husbands, and where enslaved men and women sought to seize freedom on their own terms, in both incremental and dramatic ways. The letters between Nancy and William Whatley illustrate these themes as they shaped the lives of one white couple and their four children and thirteen enslaved laborers in rural Texas. Yet this correspondence illuminates not just the vicissitudes of wartime life for the Whatleys, but also a whole world of wartime turmoil and suffering, and an end to one society and the dawn of a new one.

—JACQUELINE JONES

EDITOR'S INTRODUCTION

From May through December of 1862, Nancy Falkaday Watkins
Whatley (1837–1862) and William Jefferson Whatley (1831–1866)
chronicled in forty extant letters the Civil War experiences of a slaveholding family from the village of Caledonia in Rusk County, Texas.
The Whatley plantation was located about one hundred and thirty
miles east of Dallas and seventy-three miles from Shreveport. Nancy
wrote to her husband from their home in Caledonia, and William, to
her, from central and southeastern Arkansas, where he served as a
private in the Seventeenth Texas Cavalry organized and recruited in
1862 from the northeastern Texas counties.[1]

The Whatleys exchanged love letters, lamenting their separation.
Nancy kept William current about their four small children—John,
Archie, Jane, and Nannie, all under the age of eight—who missed
their "pa" as much as their mother did. She alternated piercing affection with urgent business questions that illustrated the stress of her
new responsibilities for all aspects of their family's affairs. Nancy's
loneliness and depression magnified the personal significance of
William's letters to her. Her Texan contemporary Lizzie Neblett
perhaps said it best about the overwhelming importance to these
women of written communion with their husbands: "I must have
someone to tell my troubles to . . . my safety valves . . . the mirrors
of my heart."[2]

Nancy Falkaday Watkins and William Jefferson Whatley married
in Rusk County in 1853; she was sixteen years old, and he, twenty-
two. In the late eighteenth century, their ancestral families were vir-

The East Texas–Arkansas region in 1862. *Map by Mary Lee Eggart.*

tual neighbors after migrating from Tidewater Virginia into adjacent counties on the Virginia–North Carolina line. The Watkinses settled in Halifax County, Virginia, and the Whatleys in Granville County, North Carolina. The area was tobacco country above the fall line of the Dan River and accessible to the Carolina and Wilderness Roads, which funneled migration into Georgia and Tennessee. From common ground these restless, land-hungry, and upwardly mobile families embarked upon their separate treks to East Texas. The cotton gin had ignited an irresistible boom fueled by the insatiable demand for raw cotton for England's burgeoning textile industry. Georgia and the territories of Alabama and Mississippi succumbed rapidly to cotton monoculture. Enmeshed in the clamor to acquire additional land and slaves to grow more cotton, the Whatleys gravitated south into northwestern Georgia and then to Alabama at about the same time as the Watkinses' passage to north-central Tennessee.[3]

Around 1805, Jesse Jernigan Watkins (1776–1837), Nancy's grandfather and the son of a Revolutionary War soldier, migrated from Halifax County to Clarksville, Tennessee, north of Nashville and east of the Cumberland River. From there, Jesse again moved the family west across the Tennessee River to Henderson County. By 1809, he had married Mary White McCorkle; their first son, Archibald H. Watkins (1812–1881), was born in Clarksville. In the early 1830s, Jesse set off with his family for Texas and its abundant land. The Watkinses were fortunate to migrate prior to the Texas Revolt of 1836 and the Panic of 1837. The latter wreaked havoc upon debtors, strangling credit, and stifling movement to Texas until after the Mexican War of 1846.[4]

In 1833 Jesse Watkins and his family illegally entered northeast Texas, ignoring Mexico's recent law forbidding migration from the United States. Initially, they camped in the future Red River County, about as far as they could get from the authority of the Mexican government.[5] There, Jesse and twenty-year-old Archibald founded the first of several Cumberland Presbyterian churches.[6] Soon, Jesse ventured south to settle near Nacogdoches, where he developed a friendship with Sam Houston, who appointed him an Indian commissioner. In November 1837, en route to negotiate the removal of the Kichai, Tawakoni, and Caddo tribes, Jesse Watkins was ambushed and killed by a band of Cherokees near present-day Dallas.[7]

By 1836, Archibald Watkins resided in Mt. Enterprise in what would become Rusk County. That same year, he crossed the porous border into the United States and returned to Tennessee to marry Mary Ann Hendrick.[8] After the birth of Nancy Falkaday Watkins in 1837, the couple returned to Rusk County and finally settled in the village of Murval, about ten miles east of Henderson. Archibald Watkins lived in Rusk County for the duration of his life and was a devoted parent and grandfather, farmer, Cumberland Presbyterian minister, first chief justice (county judge) of the newly incorporated Rusk County, Murval's United States postmaster (1853), and an owner of slaves and land.[9]

The Whatleys were on the move at the same time as the Watkinses. William Jefferson Whatley's great-grandfather Shirley Whatley (1698–1779) had migrated from Hanover County, Virginia, to Granville County, North Carolina. At Shirley's death, the estate, including slaves, was divided between his wife, Rebekka, and their children; he bequeathed five shillings each to his children of a first marriage to Mary Courtney Cherry. Shirley cites son Wilson in his will as the vanguard of the family's resettlement in the new cotton country of Georgia. Wilson explored, surveyed, and claimed new land in Wilkes County, attracting Shirley Whatley's other sons into the northwestern Georgia counties. Ornan was the exception; he ventured into Alabama. Seaborn Jones Thornton Whatley (1803–1871), William Jefferson's father, followed brother Ornan and settled in Greene County, Alabama, the birthplace in 1831 of William Jefferson Whatley. His aunt, Mary Ann (1809–1898), married John Strong of Georgia, and in 1849 they joined the surge of post–Mexican War migration to Texas.[10] The Strongs established themselves in Rusk County; their letters to Alabama must have alerted young William to the prospects in East Texas of abundant, cheap land and safety for slaveholders. In the early 1850s, William merged with the hordes of land-hungry Tennesseans and Alabamans who were "Gone to Texas." By 1853, at age twenty-two, William had arrived in Rusk County and married Nancy Falkaday Watkins.

In the decade before the Civil War, Rusk County almost doubled its population; its slave population tripled. By 1860 it was Texas's most populous county.[11] Organized in 1843 around the county seat of Henderson, Rusk County largely consisted of communities like Caledonia where life revolved around family, slaves, fields, churches, and cemeteries. There, with slave labor, Nancy and William Whatley farmed several parcels of land, producing enough cotton to gin—twenty bales in 1860—and cultivated a variety of other crops along with hog raising.[12] Ownership of thirteen slaves made them substantial people remote from the planter elite. Six of their slaves were over the age of ten, and the rest ranged from two to seven years old.

In 1860, Henderson's town center burned to the ground, and its citizens rushed to lynch Unionist Green Herndon, a fellow citizen and slave owner. One of Herndon's slaves had denounced him in public as the fire's perpetrator. Henderson's citizenry summarily hanged him and the enslaved informer. The Henderson fire and lynching of Green Herndon was just one episode in the infamous North Texas hysteria of 1860, the "Texas Troubles," which roused community after community to persecute imagined cabals of alien abolitionists and local Unionists conspiring to incite slave revolts.[13] Fantasies of slaves rebelling and massacring whites were a long-standing, deep-seated Southern and Texan phobia suddenly become reality and exacerbated by the turbulent politics of the 1850s. During that decade, the Colorado County "rebellion" of 1856 was the only event in Texas remotely like a slave insurrection. While easily suppressed, it resonated powerfully with North Texas's pandemic extremism already intensified by inflammatory accounts of Bleeding Kansas, Harpers Ferry, John Brown, and other divisive events. The stage was set for the Texas Troubles.[14]

A Rusk County historian recorded the atmosphere in Henderson and the paranoia of its leading citizens: "A committee [from Henderson] of fifty-two of the best citizens of the town and county . . . have been in closed session and correspondence with the neighboring counties . . . they believe that emissaries [exist] throughout the state, directly under control of the Abolition Aid Society of the North . . . their object is to produce a well digested plan, which by fire and assassination will finally render life and property insecure, and the slave by constant rebellion, a curse to the master."[15] The ubiquitous North Texas fires spurred ferocious persecutions of slaves, Unionists, and outsiders. Lynching was the familiar and convenient means for communities to inflict quick punishment, a hoary custom long practiced in the backcountry.[16] In October of 1862, North Texas violence peaked in Gainesville, Cooke County; local vigilantes hanged at least forty suspected Unionists.[17]

The Henderson fire's real culprits were the harsh drought of 1860, that summer's extremely hot days, and the widespread use of the new, self-igniting phosphorus matches.[18] But the lethal atmosphere created by the Texas Troubles abetted the secessionist movement whose opportunistic leaders, like Senator Louis Wigfall, exploited the hysteria to mobilize the decisive vote for Texas to secede and become the Confederacy's seventh state. Mostly migrants from Tennessee and Alabama, the white, male citizens of Rusk County voted overwhelmingly to leave the Union and flocked to the call for volunteers to fill out the new regiments forming all over East Texas in 1861.

After her husband's departure in 1862 as part of the Seventeenth Texas Cavalry, Nancy Whatley took on the management of a sizable operation and the oversight of six or seven working slaves and their children in addition to full-time domestic responsibilities and the care of her four small children. Southern women doing men's work became the norm during the Civil War years, eroding sectional paternalism and undermining women's generations-old protected status. They were now doing the work of their husbands plus their own.[19]

Nancy's letters are a narrative of East Texas life during 1862, paralleling similar female accounts of that era. Most memoirists, such as Mary Chesnut, Kate Stone, and Mary Pugh, were from substantial planter families a world away from Nancy's. She was alone, immobile, and trapped in rural Caledonia. She rarely encountered anyone other than her children and the Watkins family, difficult neighbors, and the enslaved families. Dr. Watkins's and sister Jane's visits were special events. Once in 1862, Nancy traveled a few miles from home to attend a "meeting," a local revival with the attraction of well-known itinerant preachers. Revivals afforded country people opportunities to accept Christ, to get a reprieve from daily responsibilities, and to visit with neighbors and relations.[20]

Despite the disparate backgrounds of the two women, Nancy Whatley's letters complement those of Mary Boykin Chesnut. In 1981, C. Vann Woodward explained the significance of Chesnut's letters: "She is remembered . . . for the vivid picture she left of a society in the throes of its life-and-death struggle. . . . The enduring value of the work . . . lies in the life and reality with which it evokes the chaos and complexity of a society at war."²¹ These memorable women lived in separate spheres and represented the extremes of their class, but they both reflected upon the theme of the "chaos and complexity of a society at war." Mary was a friend of Varina Davis, spouse of Confederate president Jefferson Davis. Chesnut, the ultimate insider, described the comings and goings of the inner circles of Richmond and Charleston. For Nancy, family survival consumed every waking moment. Mary attended Richmond balls and communed with Confederate leaders and discussed the great events of the conflict. Nancy yearned for a new dress and for William's imminent return. She pleaded with him to send her "cards," the scarce tools required to prepare the wool for his new shirt. Mary's lofty social position gave her the distance to critique slavery occasionally, whereas Nancy lived in close proximity to her slaves and had to work them efficiently. Both women were keenly alert to the disintegration of Southern life and agonized over their children's future. Taken together, the chronicled experiences of these women lead us to a deeper understanding of the changes that confronted and deeply troubled Southern women during the Civil War. A noteworthy difference between the two lies in the immediacy of Nancy's observations; they come down to us as a time capsule of 1862. Mary edited her letters for years after the war.²²

Nancy's letters richly detailed the fabric of East Texas rural life during the Civil War. Beleaguered by new and unfamiliar responsibilities, she wrote compellingly to her husband about her burdens. Not an overt social critic like Chesnut or the displaced Louisiana planter Kate Stone, Nancy nevertheless leaves us with a vivid picture of changing social and economic conditions.²³ She concentrated on sustaining her children, the family's land, and their slaves. She peppered William with business and management questions and kept him current on decisions. The ordeal drained her both physically and emotionally, as life in remote Caledonia sealed her off from social activities accessible to town and planter women. Drew Gilpin Faust describes the web of urban women's associations: hospital and nursing work, the Homespun Movement, the innumerable flag and sewing groups, and, of course, the churches.[24] Country isolation insulated Nancy from the social life practiced by urban Southern women.

Ownership of thirteen slaves placed the Whatleys above the median of Texas slave owners, between yeomen and the planter elite. In 1860, according to Randolph B. Campbell's analysis, the Whatley cohort, about 17.5 percent of Texan slaveholders, owned between ten and nineteen slaves, amounting to 25 percent of Texas's enslaved individuals. The planter class—about 11.4 percent of Texas slave owners—held 46 percent of the slave population.[25] Thirteen enslaved people represented the Whatleys' most valuable property.

In his letters, William sternly lectured Nancy on slave management in reductionist language that diminished the enslaved's identities and reduced them to commodities, precisely defining their status. The thirteen Whatley slaves emerge from the correspondence as shadowy, background figures known only by their first name or, collectively, as "the Negroes," but Marshall, a senior slave, was the exception. He leaps out from these pages as a rebellious, inchoate man when he confronts neighbor Mr. Miller, deputized by William to be Nancy's slave overseer.[26] Marshall's experience gives us a clue what it was like for enslaved women and men to probe for freedom, taking unspeakable risks. When referring to their slaves as "Negroes," William and Nancy were in line with the euphemistic language practiced by slave owners when referring to their property. Such usage appeared as early as the Constitutional Convention when James Madison deferred to his Southern colleagues and sanitized the final draft of the Constitution, transforming "slave" into "person" in the Three-Fifths Clause and fugitive slaves into "person[s] held to service or labor."[27] Seventy-five years later, the Whatleys habitually referred to their enslaved as "the Negroes." Exactly once in these letters William wrote the word "slave."

After her husband trooped off to Arkansas, Nancy was tested in many ways; slave management was the most demanding. Mr. Miller failed as overseer and forced Nancy into that additional role. By 1862, slaves had begun to challenge historic controls (see Marshall's confrontation of Miller). Such incidents unsettled historically insecure slave owners in Rusk County, who harbored vivid memories of John Brown, the Henderson fire, and the Texas Troubles.

In his letters from Arkansas, William harangued and threatened the family's slaves and demanded punishments. His punitive admonitions exemplified the autocratic master, and the whip represented his scepter of power.[28] As he commanded Marshall to obey, William elided into bewildered outrage that the "Negroes" didn't understand his "we are in this together" stance—as if slaves and master were partners in the struggle to preserve slavery, white supremacy, and that a Confederate victory might deliver some positive gains for enslaved people. In a revelatory passage, William declared his version of the master-slave relationship:

> . . . tell the Negroes that if they don't go ahead with their work and do right and behave themselves while I am gone that I will certainly call them to an account when I come home, and I may be there before they look for me. I am having a harder time than any of them and if they won't behave themselves and work while I am gone that they need not expect any favors from me. Tell Marshal that I will hold him accountable for his bad conduct. I told him to stay at home and see to everything about the place and if he wants to call me master any longer that he had better do it.[29]

William defaulted to the paternalistic, white supremacist ideology hastily cobbled together by Southern proslavery apologists threatened by the abrupt emergence in the 1830s of militant Northern abolitionism with its persistent demands for immediate, uncompensated emancipation. William Lloyd Garrison drummed incessantly on this theme in the pages of his *Liberator*, which aroused and rallied literate Northern elites and fueled anxieties in the South. Charles Sellers described the transformation: "Northern liberal capital turned against the anachronistic planter capital impeding its political economy, and the antinomian doubts impeding its cultural hegemony were quelled by vanguard abolitionism."[30] The embattled slavocracy countered swiftly and produced a heavily Christian, white supremacist, and paternalistic credo grounded in scripture and historic precedents, an ideology that extolled the superiority of Southern aristocratic culture over Northern commercialism. Slaveholding Southerners settled comfortably into the fiction that their version of forced labor benefited enslaved people and protected them from the alternative of wage labor in Northern textile mills.[31]

In Lower South cotton monoculture, masters controlled the enslaved and extended their productivity with a "pushing system" based upon rigorous picking and hoeing goals for individual slaves and the certainty of severe punishment for lowered productivity or aberrant behavior—the Lower South's variation on the factory system.[32] Alabama immigrants like William Whatley carried that concept of labor control to Texas, but the pushing system did not transfer effectively from Alabama work camps to the exigencies of small-scale agriculture in East Texas. Nancy, now the de facto overseer, could not stay in one place to drive her slaves because the small plantation required the enslaved workers to be deployed at separate tasks in different areas throughout the property. Supervision became more complicated, probably requiring Nancy to be on horseback, on the move and certainly ever watchful. She dealt directly with and lived in close proximity to the slaves and depended on them. That vulnerable closeness limited her capacity to be harsh. While William could resort to the whip, Nancy probably could not.

When the men delegated management to their wives, the disciplining of slaves changed, another indicator of slavery in flux. Further complicating the mistress–master slave relationship was the expanding impact of the Union Army. Wherever it invaded, Union soldiers refused to enforce the Fugitive Slave Law in occupied areas of the South, instead confiscating the enslaved as contraband of war and soon freeing, employing, and by 1862, enlisting them to fight.[33] Confiscation was in the air, and the word spread rapidly through both white and slave networks, inciting white fears and stirring hopes among the enslaved. By 1862 Union commanders had the Confiscation Acts and the Militia Act for guidelines, giving form to an evolving process.[34] The Militia Act allowed for enlistment of male slaves into the Union Army, and within about eleven months General Ulysses S. Grant committed the Ninth Louisiana Infantry (African Descent) to defend positions at Milliken's Bend against Walker's

Texas Division, which included men from Harrison County in East Texas.[35] Meanwhile in Rusk County, Nancy witnessed the spectacle of refugee planter wives and overseers driving their slaves in flight from the Union Army, foreshadowing the demise of slavery. "Refugeed" slaves in their midst was a jarring reminder to East Texans that slavery could not survive without the vigilant protection of the police powers of the states.

The Whatleys recorded intense social and economic disruptions, but the Confederacy managed to get the mails delivered with surprising efficiency, often supplemented by Rusk County neighbors and relatives and furloughed comrades who traveled between East Texas and Arkansas. The Whatleys repeatedly grumbled about the dearth of essential goods, particularly of the "cards" required for the domestic preparation of cotton and wool for a warm shirt for William and to achieve independence from Northern finished goods. The dire shortage of cards highlights a common Confederate vulnerability; women were to weave to beat the Yankees but lacked the tools to do so. The vagaries of the tobacco supply concerned William. Scarcity of paper magnified the value of each letter.

Confederate strategy upended cotton markets.[36] In 1861, the Confederate Congress rushed through the Embargo Act to freeze cotton exports and deny Britain and France access to the Lower South's cotton, their major source, confidently anticipating that the world's dominant powers would swiftly intervene to broker a truce or peace and revive the cotton market. Lincoln aggressively responded by invading and dominating the Mississippi River and its tributaries while blockading or capturing the Lower South's major ports, closing down most of the international cotton trade. The British and French demurred on intervention, and bales accumulated in New Orleans and Memphis and became valuable Union contraband. The Union further constricted exports by capturing Galveston in October 1862. Confederate general John B. Magruder regained it on January 1, 1863, and a later stalemate at Sabine Pass secured the upper reaches of the Sabine River, but the blockade continued. Cotton grown east of the Brazos River stayed in East Texas; west of the Brazos River, a secure exit for a trickle of Texas cotton was established through

Bagdad, Mexico, downstream from Matamoros at the mouth of the Rio Grande River.

Nancy had a difficult time getting her cotton ginned. As a small grower and a woman, she had to wait in line behind larger planters while labor shortages and a disappearing market promoted further delay. In addition, the Confederate currency system probably undercut the real estate market as Nancy tried to dispose of their land.

However garrulous his commentaries on camp life, in his letters William easily shifted into focused instructions on farm business and pressed for a detailed accounting of affairs at home. In his urgency to be informed, William often patronized Nancy. Finally, he could no longer discount her appeals; she persuaded him, for her peace of mind, to liquidate their homeplace and situate her and the children near the Watkins family in Murval. Meanwhile, William, ever the Jacksonian, anticipated building the family's postwar fortunes in Limestone County.

William's arrangements for male neighbors to assist Nancy in managing the operations began to collapse shortly after his departure. When she complained to him about the unreliability of Mr. Martin, William urged her acceptance: "Mr. Martin promised me when I left that he would attend to my business and do the best he could, and I am very sorry to hear that [he] is becoming negligent, if such is the case, but I do hope my dear wife that you will pause and reflect and consider well your condition. You must not expect too much at his hands. You must be cool and considerate and not suffer your passions to rise above a level. Surely he will do right."[37]

The neighbors ignored major tasks, such as getting the cotton ginned or repairing Nancy's well. Martin figured prominently in Nancy's narrative, and she regularly railed on his neglect and rudeness. He was an accomplished evader of conscription, but Nancy ignored his lack of zeal for the cause. She wanted help and had no time or energy for patriotism. Martin exhausted her patience, and, finally, on October 19, she poured out her feelings: "He [Martin] has not acted the gentleman & I will never respect him . . . for no gentleman would talk to A lady as he did to me & I told him so. It was only about my hogs getting into his field. I had sent the negroes three times to fix the cross fence [later she fixed it]. . . . Mr. Martin tore my hogs up with the dogs & beat them. . . . He is the only man that I ever wanted you to thrash."

Ultimately, Nancy had to rely on her own intelligence, knowledge, and family. Regularly, Dr. Watkins rode over from Murval to check on her; he corresponded with William about disposing of their homeplace and settling their debts. Several times Nancy mentions visits from her sister Jane.

Throughout 1862, as Nancy agonized over what to do with the slaves, her father negotiated an exit from Caledonia's burdens. Both he and William advised her to hire out the slaves to their creditors to ease their debts.[38] From summer on, hiring out was a frequent topic in the letters, and though it was common practice among slave owners, Nancy ultimately did not hire out their slaves. The influx of Louisiana and Mississippi slaves had glutted the labor market.

With a small plantation to manage and a young family to care for, one might ask why William Whatley volunteered, ten months after the post–Fort Sumter euphoria.[39] Much has to be inferred. Confederate soldiers fought for home, property, and honor.[40] To be conscripted was dishonorable, but William accepted a bounty for enlisting. In 1861, a thirty-year-old with a family deferred the call for volunteers to younger, single men.[41] The second call for volunteers under the Conscription Act of 1862 carried the draft threat. In addition, the Union invasion of northwestern Arkansas in early 1862 was a potential danger to East Texas. William enlisted to fight for his "rights" and rarely wrote a letter without a Patrick Henryesque proclamation of them. Confederate men frequently identified their cause with the American Revolution, selectively. In growing up among Alabama's Scots-Irish, William could not have missed their fierce attachment to the personal rights of white male property holders. William emerged as a second-generation Jacksonian, a man on the make for whom "rights" translated into passionate, often violent attachment to economic and social opportunity. In coming to Texas, William was following the example of John C. Calhoun, who like Shirley Whatley, had sent his son into the undeveloped Lower South to open up new land for his family and expand the slave empire.

Cumberland Presbyterianism's emphasis upon individual independence and self-reliance in finding Christ reinforced William's natural-rights convictions. In addition to implying what moved William to enlist, his own words link Confederate patriotism with dedication to fight for his slaves, land, and family. Defending rights invariably meant fighting for them. Nancy broached the subject of buying a substitute as allowed by the Conscription Act of 1862. The Whatleys were short of the twenty-slave provision of the act that exempted planters. Nancy was a reluctant patriot and ignored William's recurring assertions of his rights. She wanted him home as soon as possible, but this father of four young children made it clear that he intended to remain in place, defend his rights, and serve the Confederacy: "some conscripts have paid . . . for substitutes. For my part I expect to remain here and battle for my rights and go wherever the confederacy demands my services. I would like very much to be with you and my children but home is not home . . . without my rights and liberty."[42]

Southern white men of 1861–65 fought to preserve slavery and white supremacy. Slavery was a positive, fundamental, and self-evident right sanctioned by Christianity and the ever-evolving proslavery ideology proclaiming white supremacy. William never explicitly asserted slavery's preservation as a reason for fighting, but he didn't need to. Slave ownership and white supremacy anchored Southern culture, and the right to own humans was deeply embedded in white Southerners. William would fight to retain the right to a highly portable property vastly more valuable than land; slaves were the basis for the credit system and collateral for the slave empire's expansion. Their six or seven very young slaves were the future capital to finance his intended move west to Limestone County at the war's end. The system favored William; an upwardly mobile character like him would have fought to preserve the opportunity to add more slaves to the thirteen that he already owned. Submitting to the Union meant relinquishing the slave labor system, and this would, in turn, have imperiled Southern capital, slavery, and white supremacy—a catastrophe for the Whatleys.[43]

By May of 1862, Private Whatley and the Seventeenth Texas Cavalry

Civil War Arkansas, including locations and dates of engagements.
Map by Mary Lee Eggart.

had traveled the well-worn route to Arkansas. The Trans-Mississippi Command soon ordered the Seventeenth Texas to dismount and send their horses home.[44] They became "foot cavalry." The overgrazed, picked-over Arkansas countryside could not supply sufficient forage for the numerous Texas cavalry units. About 60 percent of Texan volunteers started their Civil War service as cavalry, and divorcing a Texan from his mount was very close to a violation of rights. The dismounting order incited sporadic resistance and mutinies in several Texan regiments.

Aside from sending his horse home and joining the ranks of the dismounted, William gave early accounts of military service that read like a resort brochure. Initially, his soldiering was an undemanding series of moving camps, long on daily tedium, short on action and glory, and reminiscent of the enlisted man's ancient plaint: "Hurry up and wait." He ruminated about the food and repeatedly instructed Nancy on childrearing, the urgency of educating John, slave management, and planting crops on time. He included news from other camps, kept her current on his health, and relayed rumors of victories and hopes for a truce or peace. Life in camp centered on his mess group, five or six men—boys, he called them—who cooked and ate together.[45]

During much of 1862, the Seventeenth camped in the vicinity of Little Rock, where William enjoyed fellowship with his messmates. He bragged to Nancy about eating well and that his health was "never better." Like so many Confederate soldiers, he optimistically anticipated British recognition of Confederate nationhood, which would force a truce to end the war.[46] In 1862, rumors of peace and imminent British and French intervention circulated throughout the camp.

The Seventeenth Cavalry was there to support the Trans-Mississippi Department's desperate efforts to keep Arkansas in the Confederacy. In the spring of 1862, Union general Samuel Curtis penetrated northwestern Arkansas.[47] On March 7–8, at Pea Ridge near Bentonville, the two armies collided, with Curtis's forces overwhelming General Earl Van Dorn's Confederates.[48] Van Dorn hastily fled the battlefield for Mississippi, leaving Arkansas unprotected and vulnerable to Union domination.[49] At this dispiriting time for Confederate Arkansas, the newly arrived Texas units reinforced the disparate forces assembled by General Thomas Hindman, Van Dorn's successor.[50] Intent on repelling Curtis, Hindman rallied what troops and support he could, including guerrilla groups, to harass Union invaders. Meanwhile, Curtis pressed southeast toward Little Rock and William's dismounted Seventeenth. Encountering resistance near Searcy, Curtis prudently veered to the east and established his base at Helena on the Mississippi River. Although Hindman was sacked in August from his Trans-Mississippi command, he remained active on the battlefield until defeated in early December of 1862 at Prairie Grove in Washington County; this small battle secured northwestern Arkansas for the Union.

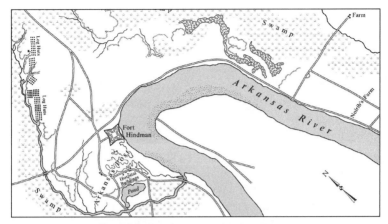

Arkansas Post. *Map by Mary Lee Eggart.*

Southeast of Little Rock, threats of Union invasion up the Arkansas River had compelled Hindman to defend Arkansas Post, where he concentrated about four thousand soldiers, including the Seventeenth.[51] About forty miles northwest of the junction of the Arkansas and Mississippi rivers, Arkansas Post occupies an unusually complex terrain of rivers, streams, bayous, and swamps. A hastily constructed fort was named after Hindman, and General Thomas Churchill and his men awaited assaults from Union army and naval forces moving up the Arkansas River.[52]

On January 11, 1863, after two days of heavy bombardment, Union forces assaulted Fort Hindman, which surrendered that afternoon, perhaps from confusion in the Confederate command structure, leaving the Texans outraged and wanting to continue the fight. William escaped captivity, but the fate of most of the Seventeenth was an Illinois prison camp. That Illinois contingent was shortly moved to Virginia and paroled; most joined the Army of Tennessee and compiled an impressive battle record, surrendering to General William T. Sherman at Durham Station, North Carolina, on April 26, 1865. William remained with the western remnants of Taylor's regiment, which was consolidated with the Eighteenth Texas Cavalry (Dismounted) and posted to Fort Alston, Louisiana, before returning to active service.[53] The high point for the western remnant of the Seventeenth came in April 1864 near Mansfield, Louisiana, as part of Polignac's Brigade. The Confederate victory at Mansfield kept Union soldiers out of northeast Texas and preserved the trade route through Mexico. William was among the handful of survivors of the often-consolidated Seventeenth who surrendered at Galveston on June 3, 1865.

Back in Caledonia, throughout 1862, Nancy vigilantly cared for her children while contending with the drought, uncertain crops, rampant hogs, restless slaves, unreliable neighbors, getting the cotton ginned, going for salt, agonizing about disposing of the home-place, and more. In her letters she bemoaned the shortage of cards and needles. And she implored William to find her a new dress in Little Rock.

Confederate women of the slaveholding class were expected to seamlessly maintain family affairs, and, like William, their spouses often didn't sympathize with or understand the stressful alterations inherent in the abrupt shift from being a protected, weak, and vulnerable species into critical decision-makers. In his first letter to her, William urged her to "nerve up." Immersed in the immediacies of daily life, Nancy rarely related or inquired about war news. One letter to her brother referred to the fall of Fort Donelson and hinted at the futility of the Cause. With her husband, she did not question the war until a letter late in 1862 where she agonized about her children's future: "Poor children, they are seeing their happiest times now. They do not know the sad realities they will have to encounter in after life which will be sure to come sooner or later."[54] Nancy worried about Union invasion from the east, "Jayhawker" raids from Missouri and Kansas, and slave rebellion at home.[55]

Above all other matters, "health" was the era's universal, immediate anxiety, adding a sobering tone to most of the Whatleys' letters. Of the forty letters, thirty-one mention health matters in the first ten or fifteen lines. Ever anxious about her children, Nancy fretted incessantly about the well-being of their extended family and the "country." She couldn't allow herself to become ill because she had to care for her children. Hardly a letter went by without news of the "health of the country" as she recounted the illnesses and deaths of family, friends, and neighbors. William kept her informed about health in the army and of Rusk County men there. In his first letter home, he described a measles epidemic in camp, a visit to the hospital, and then to a graveyard.

The Civil War determined the fate of the Whatleys—loss of property and stability of place. Despite the uncertainties of daily life during the war, Nancy and William maintained an intense love for each other; they shared this affection to the conclusion of their abbreviated lives. Their life together ended abruptly with Nancy's death on December 26. She was twenty-five and died nursing her measles-stricken children.

The Whatley letters tell a complex and stirring story of a family and society in crisis. While the men did the waiting and fighting, women like Nancy assumed unprecedented responsibilities and filled unfamiliar roles. Her experiences exemplify the disrupted lives of Southern women abruptly responsible for maintaining their fragile domestic economies in a context where all were stretched to the maximum to scratch out the necessities to wage a modern war to preserve slavery.

Nancy's narrative dominates these letters, but our only tangible memory of her is a gravestone at Pine Grove Cemetery while her husband slipped into Henderson's legend, remembered for the shotgun he used in 1864 as a participant in the Battle of Mansfield, Louisiana.

NOTES

1. Caledonia is located in the corner of southeastern Rusk County and was settled by as early as 1828. It received a post office in 1851 that continued until 1866. Its population peaked in 1880 at 150. Today, Caledonia is merely a crossroads with a single Methodist church.

2. Quoted in Drew Gilpin Faust, *Mothers of Invention: Women of the Slaveholding South in the American Civil War* (Chapel Hill: University of North Carolina Press, 1996), 118.

3. For the impact of the cotton gin, see Edward E. Baptist, *The Half Has Never Been Told: Slavery and the Making of American Capitalism* (New York: Basic Books, 2014), 94; Sven Beckert, *Empire of Cotton: A Global History* (New York: Knopf, 2014), 103–5; Adam Rothman, *Slave Country: American Expansion and the Origins of the Deep South* (Cambridge, MA: Harvard University Press, 2005), 183–85.

4. For the influence of the Panic of 1837 upon migration into Texas, see Andrew J. Torget, *Seeds of Empire: Cotton, Slavery, and the Transformation of the Texas Borderlands, 1800–1850* (Chapel Hill: University of North Carolina Press, 2015), 195–97, 211–12, 216, 261.

5. Much of the Watkins family information is based on "Nacogdoches County Families," *Texas Sesquicentennial* (Nacogdoches, TX: Nacogdoches County Genealogical Society, 1985), 686–88.

6. On the schisms within the Presbyterian Church that shaped the formation of the Cumberland Presbyterian Church in 1810, see John B. Boles, *The Great Revival: Beginnings of the Bible Belt* (Lexington: University Press of Kentucky, 1996), 159–63. The Cumberland Presbyterian Church adhered to a revisionist Calvinism—a return to original, fundamental, New Testament Christianity, emphasizing an individual's direct relationship with Christ.

7. Cecil Harper Jr., "Watkins, Jesse," *Handbook of Texas Online,* accessed November 12, 2017, http://www.tshaonline.org/handbook/online/articles/fwaac.

8. Archibald H. Watkins was always referred to as "Dr.," presumably in deference to his training in theology and perhaps also in medicine.

9. According to the 1860 Census, Dr. Watkins cultivated 60 acres of improved land, held 135 unimproved acres, and produced 100 bales of cotton.

10. Mary Elizabeth Whatley Jones, *Whatley Grandfathers Revised (The Ornan Whatley Line): Including Biographies of Heard and Crook Ancestors* (1973; Abilene, TX: self-pub., 1990), 40.

11. Virginia Knapp and Megan Biesele, "Rusk County," *Handbook of Texas Online,* accessed November 14, 2017, http://www.tshaonline.org/handbook/online/articles/hcr12.

12. United States Agricultural Census of 1860.

13. Randolph B. Campbell, *An Empire for Slavery: The Peculiar Institution in Texas, 1821–1865* (Baton Rouge: Louisiana State University Press, 1989), 184–85.

14. See Donald E. Reynolds, *Texas Terror: The Slave Insurrection Panic of 1860 and the Secession of the Lower South* (Baton Rouge: Louisiana State University Press, 2007).

15. Dorman H. Winfrey, *A History of Rusk County, Texas* (Waco: Texian Press, 1961), 40.

16. Arthur Herman, *How the Scots Invented the Modern World* (New York: Random House, 2001), 237. Lynch "law"—local vigilante justice—was practiced and refined in the late eighteenth century on the Carolina frontiers and in western Virginia and carried forward in the settling of the Lower South and Texas, where the custom flourished.

17. Richard B. McCaslin, "Great Hanging at Gainesville," *Handbook of Texas Online,* accessed November 14, 2017, http://www.tshaonline.org/handbook/online/articles/jig01.

18. Clarence L. Mohr, *On the Threshold of Freedom: Masters and Slaves in Civil War Georgia* (1986; Baton Rouge: Louisiana State University Press, 2001), 25–27. Georgia also had its fires and paranoia of abolitionist invasions and slave rebellions, and the rumors of the Texas fires confirmed apprehensions.

19. Faust, *Mothers of Invention*, 6–7.

20. See Boles, *The Great Revival*.

21. C. Vann Woodward, ed., *Mary Chesnut's Civil War* (New Haven: Yale University Press, 1981), xxvii.

22. Catherine Clinton, *Stepdaughters of History: Southern Women and the American Civil War* (Baton Rouge: Louisiana State University Press, 2016), 30.

23. Woodward, ed., *Mary Chesnut's Civil War*; John Q. Anderson, ed., *Brokenburn: The Journal of Kate Stone, 1861–1868* (Baton Rouge: Louisiana State University Press, 1955); also on Kate Stone, see Candice N. Shockley, "They Call Us All Renegades in Tyler," in Deborah M. Liles and Angela Boswell, eds., *Women in Civil War Texas: Diversity and Dissidence in the Trans-Mississippi* (Denton: University of North Texas Press), 229–58.

24. Faust, *Mothers of Invention*, 23–29, 104–6, 179–95; Vicki Betts, "'They Call It Patriotism': Homespun as Politics in the South, 1860–1861" (2002), accessed April 30, 2018, http://apps.uttyler.edu/vbetts/homespun%20patriotism.htm.

25. Campbell, *An Empire for Slavery*, 194.

26. NFW to WJW, November 9, 1862.

27. Michael J. Klarman, *The Framers' Coup: The Making of the United States Constitution* (New York: Oxford University Press, 2016), 265.

28. Baptist, *The Half Has Never Been Told*, 120–21, 141–42.

29. WJW to NFW, October 12, 1862.

30. Charles Sellers, *The Market Revolution: Jacksonian America, 1815–1846* (New York: Oxford University Press, 1991), 396.

31. On the evolution of pro-slavery ideology, see James Oakes, *Slavery and Freedom: An Interpretation of the Old South* (New York: Knopf, 1990), 174–81. Also W. J. Cash, *The Mind of The South* (New York: Alfred A. Knopf, 1941), 63, 83, 92; Bertram Wyatt-Brown, *Southern Honor: Ethics and Behavior in the Old South* (New York: Oxford University Press, 2007), 66–67.

32. Baptist, *The Half Has Never Been Told*, 116–19, 134–36.

33. For the grim conditions in the early contraband slave camps of Helena, Vicksburg, and Natchez, see James Marten, *The Children's Civil War* (Chapel Hill: University of North Carolina Press, 2000), 90, accessed via Hoopla: https://www.hoopladigital.com/title/11802849.

34. The Freedmen and Southern Society Project, History Department of the University of Maryland, Documents and Chronology of Emancipation, thoroughly outlines the unfolding process that led to the enlistment of freedmen. See http://www.freedmen.umd.edu.

35. For an account of the Battle of Milliken's Bend and the brutal treatment of African American soldiers, see George S. Burkhardt, *Confederate Rage, Yankee Wrath: No Quarter in the Civil War* (Carbondale: Southern Illinois University Press, 2007), 56–68.

36. Beckert, *Empire of Cotton*, 241–46. The chapter titled "A War Reverberates around the World" (241–73) provides a global context for the changes in cotton markets.

37. WJW to NFW, October 12, 1862.

38. On the practice of owners hiring out their slaves, see Campbell, *An Empire for Slavery*, 82–92; Paul D. Lack, "Urban Slavery in the Southwest," in Bruce A. Glasrud and James M. Smallwood, eds., *The African American Experience in Texas* (Lubbock: Texas Tech University Press, 2007).

39. On married men volunteering, see James M. McPherson, *For Cause and Comrades: Why Men Fought in the Civil War* (New York: Oxford University Press, 1997), 134–40. On later enlistees like William J. Whatley, see Kenneth W. Noe, *Reluctant Rebels: The Confederates Who Joined the Army after 1861* (Chapel Hill: University of North Carolina Press, 2010).

40. A prime source for deep analysis of Southern honor is the work of Wyatt-Brown: *Southern Honor* and *Honor and Violence in the Old South* (New York: Oxford University Press, 1986). See also McPherson, *For Cause and Comrades*, 22–26.

41. James M. McPherson, *Battle Cry of Freedom: The Civil War Era* (New York: Oxford University Press, 1988), 430–33.

42. WJW to NFW, May 31, 1862.

43. Aaron Sheehan-Dean, *Why Confederates Fought: Family and Nation in Civil War Virginia* (Chapel Hill: University of North Carolina Press, 2009), 17, accessed via Hoopla: https://www.hoopladigital.com/title/11710041, 17.

44. During August, William Whatley served with the detail that returned the Seventeenth's horses to East Texas; this accounts for the August gap in the Whatley letters.

45. William refers to his mess group several times. See B. P. Gallaway, *The Ragged Rebel: A Soldier in W. H. Parsons' Texas Cavalry, 1861–1865* (Austin: University of Texas Press, 1988), 27.

46. Beckert, *Empire of Cotton*, 259–65. On the Union blockade, cotton diplomacy, and British recognition, see McPherson, *Battle Cry of Freedom*, 382–91.

47. Union general Samuel Ryan Curtis (1805–1866) had an unusual career in that success seemed to bring demotion followed by even more challenging assignments. After he outmaneuvered Van Dorn at Pea Ridge, he spent much of the war keeping Missouri in the Union. During the 1861–62 campaign, he was criticized for freeing captured slaves and selling cotton to feed them. See the Curtis article in the online version of *The Encyclopedia of Arkansas History and Culture:* http://www.encyclopedia ofarkansas.net/encyclopedia/entry-detail.aspx?search=1&entryID=2365.

48. The Battle of Pea Ridge secured Missouri for the Union, forced a Confederate retreat to the Arkansas River, and shifted the Federal area of operations southeast into the river war.

49. After graduating from West Point, Earl Van Dorn served in the imperialist campaigns of the Mexican and Seminole Wars and numerous Texas campaigns against other Native Americans. Defeats at Pea Ridge and Corinth brought him lesser commands. His career ended in 1863 when a cuckolded husband murdered him in his tent.

50. Before the Civil War, Thomas Carmichael Hindman was a lawyer and a politician. A congressman, he was commissioned brigadier general at age thirty-three. He fought and was wounded at Shiloh. Promoted to major general, he took over the Trans-Mississippi Department after Pea Ridge and reorganized Arkansas to return to

the offensive. Soon sacked, he fought at Chickamauga, Chattanooga, and Kennesaw Mountain. Denied a pardon after the war, he fled to Mexico, returned to Arkansas, became an advocate for black suffrage, and was assassinated at his home.

51. Arkansas Post was an ancient site long before the Europeans arrived in the 1680s, when it was a Quapaw village.

52. Thomas James Churchill, a Kentuckian and attorney, served as a volunteer in the Mexican War. In 1861, he raised the First Arkansas Volunteers and fought at Pea Ridge. As commander of Arkansas Post, he surrendered Fort Hindman on January 11, 1863, and went to prison camp with many of his men. He was later elected governor of Arkansas.

The Fort Hindman/Arkansas Post expedition revealed the conflicts in the Union chain-of-command, which centered on the differences between Grant and John A. McClernand, a "political" general who had replaced Sherman. Grant was focused on Vicksburg and had ordered McClernand to move down the Mississippi River. McClernand instead went up the Arkansas River to seize Arkansas Post and then intended to move on to Little Rock. Grant ordered him back to the Mississippi and relieved him on January 30, 1863. While Fort Hindman was a victory for the Union, it had limited strategic value and was a diversion from Grant's concentration on finishing off Vicksburg.

53. The Seventeenth continued to serve in western Louisiana in the bayou actions in 1863–64. In addition to the Battle of Mansfield, there were later actions at Franklin, Natchitoches, and Sabine Crossroads.

54. NFW to WJW, November 9, 1862.

55. Jayhawkers: the roving bands of Unionists based in Kansas and Missouri who conducted their own civil war within the greater one. They rarely raided in East Texas. What Nancy Whatley probably referred to were "bushwhackers," white men who fled into the Big Thicket area of Southeast Texas and Calcasieu Parish, Louisiana, to sit out the "rich man's war." To sustain themselves, they raided regularly, widely—and indiscriminately.

NOTE ON EDITORIAL METHOD

I have transcribed the letters of Nancy Falkaday Whatley and William Jefferson Whatley from copies of the 1931 photostats duplicated from the original letters. They appear as is with occasional brackets to clarify or indicate damages and folds that obscure the text. Nancy and William Whatley wrote in a stream of consciousness with frequent, abrupt subject changes. Nancy could be recounting the death of a neighbor, then shift into a question about when to best plant corn to speculating on imminent slave rebellion then on to a tender passage of how their children missed their father. While the Whatleys were literate enough, they spelled erratically and were arbitrary about punctuation; these are single-paragraph letters. They did not write for the ages or for publication.

CAST OF CHARACTERS

(in order of appearance)

William Jefferson Whatley (WJW): Spouse of Nancy Falkaday What-ley, son of Mr. and Mrs. Seaborn Jones Thornton Whatley of Greene County, Alabama. Migrated to Rusk County about 1850–1851.

Nancy Falkaday Watkins Whatley (NFW): Spouse of William Jeffer-son Whatley, oldest child of Dr. and Mrs. Archibald H. Watkins. Born in Tennessee, 1837.

Mr. Miller: Neighbor WJW asked to serve as overseer of their slaves.

Jesse Jernigan Watkins: Led the Watkins family to East Texas from Tennessee. Settled near Nacogdoches, Texas, appointed an Indian commissioner, and killed by Cherokees in 1837.

Jesse Watkins: NFW's brother, killed in the Civil War.

Dr. Archibald H. Watkins: Son of Jesse Jernigan Watkins and father of NFW.

John Strong Whatley: Eldest son of NFW and WJW.

Mr. Martin: Neighbor designated by WJW to support NFW in man-aging their small plantation while he served the Confederate army in Arkansas.

Jane Watkins: NFW's sister.

Jane Burney Whatley: Older daughter of NFW and WJW.

Marshall (also spelled Marshal): Slave owned by NFW and WJW. Challenged their neighbor, Mr. Miller, in 1862, and gave him "saucy jaw."

Nancy Lillie/Mary Whatley: Youngest child of NFW and WJW.

Archibald Henry Whatley: Second son of NFW and WJW.

George Isham Watkins: Another brother of NFW who survived the war.

AN EAST
TEXAS
FAMILY'S
CIVIL WAR

MAY 1862

"I hope you . . . will nerve up and bear our separation with
patience and fortitude as I am battling for you."

WJW writes from Arkansas . . . Regiment already has health issues . . . Reorganization of regiment and election of officers . . . Nancy's brother Jesse is out of the hospital . . . The dead . . . Expecting Federals . . . Anxious for a fight . . . Martial law and passports.

May 23, 1862
Little Rock, Arkansas

My Dear Wife

I have concluded to write you a few lines this evening to let you know how I am getting along. Our regiment on the 20th inst arrived and found two other Texas regiments here Col Lucets and Parsons and some other Arkans troops.[1] The federals are about some 20 or so miles above here [Little Rock]. Some of Col Parsons men were out on a scout a few days since and had a fight with them, killing about thirty five and loosing three killed and five missing. I am in better health than when I left home. All the boys from my neighborhood are well except AC Thomas and John Ray. Thomas was left at Camden [Arkansas] about ten days since. Have not heard from him since. There is a good deal of sickness in our regiment, mostly measles. The men are scattered from here back home. I believe Wynne's company stands it better than any company in the regiment. We reorganized our regiment yesterday for three years under the conscript law which provides for all men over thirty five and under eighteen to go home [WJW would turn thirty-one on May 25, 1862]. So you may look for some of our neighborhood home soon. I think Mr. Landen, Dr. Attaway, and Mr. Miller will be sure to come. We have elected Capt Taylor from Cherokee [county] Col [Colonel], Hendrick Lt. Col, McClarty major. There has been several changes in the company officers. Watkins [Jesse Jernigan Watkins (1828–1911), NFW's uncle] is capt of his company instead of White. Wynne is still our capt. I have visited the hospitals here and examined the registers and find the names of a good many Texans from Jacks, Crumps and other Texas regiments and among them I saw the name of your bro Jesse [1844–1862] but found that he had returned to his regiment or left the hospital of the 30th April. I also visited the graveyard and found the graves of a great many soldiers and some acquaintances. Among them was Wm Clinton and Henry Ball from Crumps Battalion. Crumps has a great many men buried here and there are some sick here now. John Clinton had just left the hospital. Things are a little exciting here. They are expecting the federals soon and our boys seem anxious for a fight. Marshal [martial] law is proclaimed here and we are not allowed to go about without a passport. I do not know how long we will remain here but I reckon several days. We are expecting two more regiments from Texas soon and then we will probably cross the river [Arkansas] but where our destination will be I do not know. You must write to me at this place and if I should leave this country I will try and have it forwarded. You will direct your letter WJ Whatley, Little Rock Arkans, Col Taylor's regiment, company F, care of Captain Wynne. I will write to you as often as I can. I am getting anxious to hear from you and my dear little children. I hope you are well and will nerve up and bear our separation with patience and fortitude as I am battling for you. We have had some bad weather lately. It is rumored here that Locks regiment will be here soon but we hear anything in the camps but the truth.[2] I wrote you from El Dorado and will write to you again soon. Remember me to all and believe that I am as ever

your true husband

1. Colonel William Henry Parsons experienced a colorful and turbulent life of soldier, editor, and publisher in Texas. An able battlefield commander, he defended Little Rock and participated in driving Union general Nathaniel Banks from Louisiana during the Red River Campaign of 1864.

2. In November of 1862, Locke's Tenth Texas Cavalry Regiment was dismounted and sent to the Army of Tennessee. For a dramatic summary of the unit's service in numerous battles in the Trans-Mississippi, see Matthew K. Hamilton, "Tenth Texas Cavalry," *Handbook of Texas Online*, accessed November 23, 2017, http://www.tsha online.org/handbook/online/articles/qkt13.

MAY 31, 1862
WJW TO NFW

"For my part I expect to remain here and battle for my rights and go wherever the confederacy demands my services."

Private's ignorance of the big picture ... The battle near Corinth, Mississippi ... Not giving up on getting a new horse ... Discharges and buying substitutes ... Ringing statement on patriotism and rights ... Uncertainty ... Instructions to Nancy ... Admonishes John, the eldest, to keep the pigs alive ... Little Rock ... Shortage of goods ... Tell the "Negroes" to do right!

May 31, 1862
Little Rock Arkansas

My Dear Wife

As Henry Larson and Doct Attaway are going to start home today I have concluded to write you again that you may know how I am getting along. I have been suffering somewhat from [a] cold for a few days but have been able to wait on myself and have a pretty good appetite. Mr. Miller is not very well but is up and about. John Ray is dead. Evans Jo Thomas Jack Easley and Jim Mosely have the measles but I don't think they are dangerous. Al Thomas has got up well. Thad, Gus Treadwell, Stanton Hiller on balance are well. We have a great deal of sickness in our regiment and company. Hardly half are able to do duty but it is mostly measles and they are getting along as well as could be expected. Only two deaths in our regiment as yet. The enemy are in about forty miles [in the letter from May 23 it was twenty miles] of us the most of our boys who are well are out on a scout and have been for four days and we have a rumor here that they are fighting but don't know as to the truth of it. I have sold my carryall [canvas tote bag] for a hundred dollars in Confederate money. Mr. Miller will probably be discharged soon and I will send you some money by him and if we draw any money which we will probably do in a few days I will be enabled to send a hundred dollars or more. Matt Barton is here on his way home from Corinth.[1] He reports a great deal of sickness at that place. A good many of our boys are sick. Among them are the three Hopkins, Sam Phillips, Jim Furlon, and Gus and others but as Henry Lawson can tell the news I will not enumerate further though he says he didn't think any of them are dangerous. Your Brother Jesse is sick at his uncles in Memphis but not dangerous. We look for our boys in from the scout in a day or two and then I will probably have some news and if so I will write to you again. My horse is not doing very well. We don't get enough for them to eat and he is very nice about eating and drinking and frequently suffers when he can't get good corn and clear water. We don't get any fodder at all.[2] I have been tempted to sell and buy another on that account. I believe I could get a horse for less money that would stand the trip better. Milton, Ben, and Wiley Jones are here. They are in Col Parsons regiment. Ben is sick and has a discharge. Wiley has also as he is under 18 and they will probably start home in a few days. A great many have left all ready who are released by the conscript act. And some conscripts have paid from five hundred to one thousand dollars for substitutes. For my part I expect to remain here and battle for my rights and go wherever the confederacy demands my services. I would like very much to be with you and my children but home is not home with me without my rights and liberty. I am anxious to hear from you and hope I will soon. I don't know how long we will remain here but I think this place will be head quarters for some time yet. I have no idea now that we will go to Corinth. You will write to me at this place until directed otherwise and Direct to WJ Whatley, Little Rock Ark Col Taylor's regiment and Capt Wynne's company. Will Wynne has measles. You must do the best you can and advise with your father how to do who I know will be ever ready to counsel you aright. Tell the children they must be good children and mind what you tell them. Tell John he must feed the pigs and not let them die for when I come home I will want some meat. Little Rock is a very sorry looking place for a city of its size and not one bit of accommodation about the people. Goods of every description are very scarce here and worth about four prices, tobacco $1.00 a plug and not good at that. There is a confederate gunboat up here now anchored out in the [Arkansas] river which mounts three big guns two sixty-fours and one ninety pounder. B Galloway has gone home and will return soon to this place which would be a good opportunity to send a letter if you should have a chance to see him or send the letter to him. If Mr. Martin has not joined any company tell him not do so if he can help it. Write to me what has been done with my cotton.[3] [Ginner, name unreadable] must take that cotton if he hasn't already got it. He agreed to take it and he must do so. My love to all. Tell the Negroes they must go ahead and do right while I am gone and take care of everything. I often think of you and my little children. I hope and pray that the Lord will guide and protect you.

Your Husband
WJ Whatley

1. Corinth, Mississippi, was the strategically significant junction of the Ohio and Mobile and the Memphis and Charleston railroads.

2. By the spring of 1862, the Confederate Army had stripped its Arkansas sector bare of grazing for the cavalry, which hastened the conversion of many of the Texan cavalry regiments, including the Seventeenth, to dismounted foot cavalry.

3. The CSA imposed a cotton embargo in late 1861 to rouse English and French manufacturers to pressure their governments into forcing a truce, end the war, and guarantee Confederate independence. This "Cotton Diplomacy" failed ultimately to move the neutral great powers. With cotton dead on the market—unless one could get it to Bagdad, Mexico, below Matamoros at the mouth of the Rio Grande—ginners went out of business and NFW had a difficult time of it to gin her cotton. The Whatleys were captives of global economic forces beyond their understanding.

JUNE 1862

"Her pa has gone to fight the Yankees."

Bountiful corn crop . . . Mr. Martin supposed to go for salt . . . Shortage of wheat seed . . . Rumors of her brothers' deaths, doubts the credibility of the source . . . Deaths from black tongue . . . Loneliness and isolation . . . Urges WJW to write.

Caledonia Rusk Texas
June the 4 1862

My dear Husband:

I yesterday read your letter from Mr. Miller in which he said that we could write you all at Little Rock and I knew that you would be very anxious to hear from your family. I have seated myself to drop you a few lines that you may know how we all are at home. This leaves us all well at this time except two of the little Negroes have the measels. John [oldest child] has had a brush of them but he has got well. I was quite sick last week but am about well again. We are getting along pretty well. I think every person that has looked at our crop [corn] says that it is the best they have seen. I rode through it last Friday. The new ground beyond the orchard is as high as my head and me on horseback. It is so all over. The rest all looks well but that is the best now. But Pa was down last week [from Henderson].[1] He says that if the seasons hold out that the young corn will be the best that we have. We have tassels and silks in the old corn. Mr. Martin has not gone yet [i.e., been conscripted]. He says that he intends to stay until he is forced off and there has not been any movements made towards it yet. Mr. Martin and Mr. Birdwell are going to take all hands and go to make salt for us all.[2] They will be done laying by the crop by middle of next week. We have not been able to get the cotton ginned yet. It was rotting so that we moved it last week into another pen. We did not cut any wheat at all. It was a perfect failure. All of the oats were cut but they were hardly worth cutting. The barley done pretty good. Mr. Martin thinks it is hardly worthwhile to sow wheat wants to sow mostly barley but I want wheat sowed one more time if we can get seed. I was up at cousin Haydens last week and read a letter from Elijah. He was at Corinth. It was written the 27 of April. There was three fourths sick with cold, said they had been in mud and water from shoe mouth to knee deep for three weeks. Mr. Treadwell got a letter from Gustavus. He stated that both my brothers were dead, but I do not believe it or at least if it is so he has had no chance to hear it. It would not surprise me to hear that Jesse [NJW brother] was too, for he was very low with typhoid fever on the 25 of April. He was at Uncle Bankses in Memphis. Aaron [another NFW brother] was there also sick. Capt Davis is dead. He died with black tongue at Houston. A great many died there. Pa told me that Antoinette Scruggs was dead [Rusk County relative Antoinette Strong Scruggs (1834–62)]. Aunt Mary got well. Capt White stayed at Mr. Millers night before last on his way home. I am very lonesome but get along a great deal better than I expected. I am looking for Jane [NFW's sister, Jane Watkins] every day. She has not been here since you left but the school has broken up now & I hope that she will stay with me a good part of her time when they all go off to the salt mines. I think I shall go to Pa's but I do not know. I am trying to keep the hogs alive but corn has held out better than I expected but will not have quite enough I do not think. We are going to run a cross fence where the wheat was sowed & let the hogs have the pasture. I get more milk & butter than I ever did in my life. I do most heartily wish that you all had some of it as I have a fine [jar] of butter packed away waiting for an opportunity to send it to the river. I am going to try to make cheese. If I have any luck at it I will save one until you come back. I went to preaching last Sunday. The little boys weren't with me. I had a sermon from Elder Whitmore. I saw cousin Syl. He says be sure to write to him. He has been to see me. The horses of some of the boy's in Jack's regiment have come home, the worse looking objects you ever saw. Pa got all his. He brought Freedom's Horn for me to ride. Your horses are all fat. The big mule is in as good order as I ever saw him. John says that your puppies are dead but it was not because he did not attend to them. I think they died with distemper. Arch says he wants you come home. Jane very often speaks of you. She frequently wants me to nurse her because her pa has gone to fight the Yankees. I want you to write twice every month. You will say that you will have nothing to write often but anything from you will interest me. I was very glad to hear that your health was improving. The country is generally in moderate health. I hear of chills on the creeks more than anywhere else. If we are sick much I do not know what I will do but time will show whether we will be sick or not. I want you to write me what you think I had better do if Mr. Martin has to leave. Tell Thad that his mother is complaining of him for not writing to her. They are all sick. Louisa is here now & says for him to write to her. The neighborhood is well as far as I know. I want you to be sure & write to me often, very often & I will manage to pay the postage. Write to me if you will be allowed to come home on furlough or not at the end of twelve months. I could write all day to you but my paper is about out so I must close. I remain as ever

Your affectionate wife
NF Whatley

1. "Pa" was NFW's father, Dr. Archibald H. Watkins.
2. Rusk County had abundant sources of salt, including a salt works in the Henderson area. In 1862, salt became a government monopoly.

"Measels are all through the country now.
They were brought in by the soldiers."

Visiting a neighbor . . . Martin slacks on . . . Dr. Watkins solves the "going for salt" problem . . . NFW's vegetable garden . . . Measles epidemic continues . . . NFW despair . . . Fears for her family . . . Deaths of acquaintances . . . Considers hiring out the slave Marshall to pay off some debt.

June 11th 1862
Rusk Texas

To My Dearest Husband

I have seated myself this morning to drop you a few lines in answer to yours of the 31st [May] Henry Lawson got home last evening. I am now at his house. His wife sent for me yesterday morning. I shall go home this evening. This leaves all of our family well & getting along as well as could be expected in your absence. Mr. Martin has not enlisted yet & says that he is not going until he is forced to do so. It is his intention to start Monday morning to the salt saline to make salt for himself and us. He will take Tom and Marshal [two of the Whatley slaves] with him. He will finish laying by [piling soil up to support immature corn] this week. We will get about two acres of [sweet] potatoes set out this week as we shall wait for rain no longer but are watering them. We are not suffering for rain as yet, only for potatoes & [of] our gardens mine is very fine indeed have plenty of vegetables. The residents of the country are generally in moderate health. Measels are all through the country now. They were brought in by the soldiers. There were two regiments at Mt. Enterprise [ten miles from Caledonia], but they are all gone but the sick & some to nurse them. There are forty five in & around that place that are sick. I have not a doubt but that I shall get them into my family but

I hope not. I would not dread it so if there would be any one left to wait upon us but for us all to be down at once and not one able to do anything for another would be very bad. I heard from Pa's a few days since. They were all well then but expected to have the measles as there have been a good many sick soldiers there. The children think that because cousin Henry came home you can come. They stood by with a wishful eye when he was giving his children presents and seemed to think that you ought to come and bring them something too. I have them all with me. I want you to write to me whether there is anything in the way of clothes that you will need. If so let me know immediately and if I have my health you shall have it. Cousin Henry tells me that you are at least 20 or 25 lbs heavier [than] you were when you left home I was rejoiced to hear for you may rest assured that your feeble health caused me many an uneasy hour. It was hard enough to give you up to go through what you will have to go through with, in good health, but more so in the condition your health was. Mr. Johnson has not ginned your cotton yet but I intend to go by there today to see him myself and if he will not gin it immediately I shall try some other person for he has not fulfilled his promises with me now and I will not try him anymore after this. Clarke Phillips is dead. He died at Corinth. I suppose you know that Dick Young and wife were dead also. Ask Antoinette Scruggs. They have been dead some time but I did not hear until recently. Nate Lawler lost his least child last week. Also old Mrs. Rays [son] died very suddenly. If we have two more rains there will be more corn raised according to its ground planted than was ever in three years. Every person that has seen our crop says that with reasons we are good for fifteen hundred baskets. I heard that Mr. Hamlett wanted to hire hands [slave labor] to build him a dwelling house. He wants to get them from persons that owe him. I thought I would see him and let him have Marshal long enough to pay what we owe there. The most of it was for [unreadable] you know and let it go in the settlement between you and Pa. I will see what Mr. Martin says [unreadable] first. It will be the same as money to you and they [slaves] are not doing much now no how. I may err in my management and doubtless will but I am trying to do the best I can. You must write often for it gives me great pleasure to hear from you. I read and reread your letters over again until I almost learn them by heart. That the Lord may guide and protect you in the many dangerous trials through which you may be called to go is the prayer of your affectionate wife.

NF Whatley
Write as often as you can.

JUNE 13, 1862
WJW TO NFW (DAMAGED)

"They [Whatley slaves] are having a much easier time than their master."

Anxious for a letter . . . Union forces escape to the White River . . . Pay problems . . . Challenges NFW to be a better farmer . . . Mr. Martin off to war? . . . Instructions on crop planting . . . Admonishes the "negroes" to work harder . . . Closing prayer for her.

Camp Near Searcy[1]
June 13th 1862

My Dear Wife,

As I have an opportunity of sending a letter I will again drop you a few lines. This is the fourth letter I have written to you and have not received a line from you, but must believe you have written. [Note: Two out of the four letters survived and are published here.] I am very anxious to hear from you. I wrote your father a few days ago and sent the letter by a Mr. Laws who lives at London [in northwest Rusk County]. The letter will [on the fold and unreadable]. . . . I sent fifty dollars in that letter. . . . [ten lines damaged and unreadable]. . . . We have five texas regiments here and are daily expecting others. Gen Albert Rust [of Arkansas] state is our Brigadier general.[2] We have had out scouts for some time and have had two or three little skirmish fights killing a few men and capturing eight prisoners and several horses & one wagon. It is believed here now that the enemy have made good their escape on the other side of white river. I do not know how long we will stay here or where our ultimate destination will be. You will still direct your letters to Little Rock Arkansas until otherwise informed as there is no mail from here to that point and it has to be brought up by [boat]. My mess are all in good health and the most of the boys from our neighborhood. Evans, [unreadable] Fergersen and James Mosely were left sick at Little Rock but were improving when last heard from. We have not drawed any money yet nor can I tell when we will. We have been promised it ever since we left Little Rock but still I see no prospect, it is reported here that the enemy have entire possession of the Mississippi river which will make it difficult to get money from Richmond and I fear there is not enough on this side to pay us off.[3] I have a little money and will send you a few dollars by Mr. Miller when he comes whether we draw or not. He don't know yet when he will come home as he is not discharged and may have to stay out 90 days from the passage of the conscript act which will be about the middle of next month. So he will be home then if not sooner. I hope you have made a good crop as I have had account of good rains passing through eastern Texas. You can do the best you can and see if you can't beat my farming. I suppose by this time Mr martin has left for the army. I gave him full instructions about my business before I left, which was to built a crop through the field beginning at the creek where the present crop fence joins the running north through a little piece of woods not cleared up just edging the hill and [unreadable instructions] another beginning where the branch runs in to creek following the branch up to the fork [unreadable] running straight through [unreadable]. Starting the fence somewhere he [unreadable] bars and cotton pen. I want this fence put on [unreadable] of the branch next to the old bottom. The present crop fence you will have to move [unreadable] rails in making the others.

[We will divide] the farm into three fields and if you have any small grains you had best use the back field where the old orchard is. You plant the other two in corn. The new ground should be fenced and cleaned up and planted before Christmas. The negroes have time and I think they will. Tell them that. They must go ahead and do the best they can and take care of everything around the place. As I am now enlisted for three years and can't be at home and will look to them and tell them their conduct will not be forgotten by me while I am gone. If good it will be rewarded and if bad I will certainly call them to account when I get home. They must not flinch from anything except sickness for they are having a much easier time than their master. Our wagons have been cut down to one to each company, and consequently we have had to leave about half our luggage including tents, cooking utensils, blankets, and clothing. I managed to keep all my blankets and the most of my clothes. I think I have plenty left to do me very well. We have been getting plenty to eat so far but generally though our horses are doing better now than they were a short time since. Tell my little children to be good children and don't forget me. It is true I am absent far from you but yet you are watched over by a kind providence whose ears are ever open to the ones of those who diligently seek & put their trust in him. I commend you into his hands & hoping you will lay hold of the promises laid down in his hands and try and instill those principles into our little children. You must write to me. I will write to you every week or ten days if I have an opportunity.

Farewell as ever your Husband in love.
W. J. Whatley

1. Skirmishes in the Searcy area in 1862 allowed the Confederates to deflect General Samuel Curtis's attempts to take Little Rock.

2. General Albert Rust was an Arkansas politician, ardent secessionist, and Union and Confederate congressman. He served in Arkansas, Tennessee, and Louisiana.

3. Memphis fell in the second week of June 1862, which constricted east-west communications for the Confederacy and resulted in pay delays for the Confederate soldiers in Arkansas.

"The measels are scattered all through the country."

Separation pains . . . Measles from the soldiers continue . . . Rural medicine . . . Drought fear . . . Producing a lot of milk and butter . . . Ginning problems continue . . . News of her brothers . . . Desperate for goods, especially thread . . . Wants a black dress . . . Children each want a knife . . . News of cooperative slaves . . . Martin avoids conscription.

Caledonia Rusk Cty Texas

June the 20th/62

My Beloved Husband,

It is with feelings of pleasure mingled with sadness that I seat myself to write to you. I am sad because we are so far separated from each other & it is a pleasure to me to hold sweet communication with one I love if even by letter. This leaves us all well and I do hope that it will find [you] enjoying the same great blessing. The country generally is a great deal healthier than it was last year, but not as much as usual. There are a good many cases of Fever scattered through it. I was at cousin Haydens day before yesterday. He had seven cases in his family, but there was only two of them his white ones of the little boys. The measels are scattered all through the country. They left [soldiers] at Mt. Enterprise some forty five. There has several died & says that four more are sure to die. The old Doctor Ruttig took several [sick soldiers] to his house and he did not save a single one which is more than can be said for some of the rest. If they get into my family I am going to send for him & get his advice as to how to treat them and doctor them myself. He says he had as soon knock them in the head to give them calomel which the rest are doing in every case.[1] Doctor Attaway has taken the measels since he got back.

They are also at John Strange's. I think that if we do not get rain soon we will be sick. I am afraid as we have not had any rain for about four weeks until yesterday when we had a light shower, but it will be as dry as ever in a day or two if it does not rain again. It has been very warm for sometime. There are some prospects of rain this evening. Pa's folks are in tolerable health. He had one case of Fever. It was Len. Pa has made arrangements to get our salt without going & making it. He sold some cotton to buy salt with. I am very glad that he did so for I was afraid that my folks would be sick & to be sick away from home would be very bad you know. I often ask myself the question whether you are sick or well & if sick what kind of treatment you receive. I never go to the table but what I think of you & wish I knew where you are at that moment. I often wish you had some of the milk & butter I have. For we have it in abundance. We are done laying by the crop got done last week. Mr. Martin is going to put the Negroes at work fencing new ground when he gets done splitting rails. Marshal is now gone to [grist] mill. He started last Monday. He had to go to several before he could get his meal. The water mills are stopped on account of water & there is no sort of accommodation at Davis's mill. They are so busy they cannot staff hands enough to run the mill. I went to see Johnson myself about ginning your cotton. He says that he has to take a trip out West when he lays by his crop and will gin it when he comes back & gets through ginning out what there is in ahead of us. His gin house is full. I then sent Martin to see Henry. He cannot gin it before the middle of July & that will be before Johnson will be near ready. In fact Johnson said he did not want to gin it at all if I would send it anywhere else. I reckon I shall send it to Henry as I do not care to trouble Johnson about it again. I read a letter from Jack Walker. He is now in Arkn [Arkansas] come back sick. Jim passed here this morning on his way to Jefferson. John and Louis Elliott were with him. I have just read a letter from uncle Banks. It was written the 6th day of May. Jessee had got well enough to go to Uncle Jerry's, him and Aaron both. They were afraid that the Yankee's would take the place & then they would be prisoners so they left in time. Jessee is coming home as soon as he can get a discharge which will be in July. They came near dying, both of them. They were just able to walk the 10th of last month. Marshal has just got home from the mill. Pa starts after the salt next Monday. He takes my men. Mrs. Miller is looking for Mr. Miller everyday. She says tell him to bring her one bunch of thread if it is not over $5. If it is over that for him not to get it. She wants no. 10 or 12. If he could bring one for me & you could spare the money to get it I would be very glad. I want it for jeans warp & for shirts. If you could get me a dress of some kind for Sunday and meet with an opportunity of sending it. I want you to do so if you can. Please get a black one. Do get me one if you please. John [son] says you must send him a knife. Arch says send him one. Jane says she wants one too. Mary can walk around a chair and is not as fleshy as when you left.[2] I think [she] will walk soon. The children often speak of you. I read all your letters to them & they talk over the contents of one until I get another. The negroes are doing very well. I think they seem to be more careful of everything than ever were before. They are obedient & I get along with them very well. Tom will do anything that he can that I tell him and tries what he cannot go through with. In fact if they will only continue as they are now I am perfectly satisfied with them. I want you to write to me once a week or once in two weeks anyhow for reading your letters is the greatest pleasure that I enjoy now & next to reading yours is writing to you. I would be so much delighted to see you but when I think of seeing you I think of it only at the end of your first year of service but write to me soon as you receive this. I do think that I will write to you every week if I can get the paper. Martin is about to get out of going to the war. Johnson will swear that he was 26 when he came here & he has been here 9 years. The Negroes often talk about you and want to see you they say. From your ever loving wife

N. F. Whatley

1. Dr. Ruttig had good instincts about the perils of mercury-based calomel. See Glenna R. Schroeder-Lein, *The Encyclopedia of Civil War Medicine* (Armonk, NY: M. E. Sharpe, 2008), 58.

2. The Whatleys refer to their youngest child throughout their letters as Mary, perhaps a nickname. In all surviving records, her name is Nancy Lillie Whatley.

"If we do not get rain before long we will be a ruined people."

Health of the country reviewed . . . Measles continue . . . "I am in daily dread" . . . Drought and loss of corn crop . . . Martin—now he's going! . . . Dr. Watkins's counsel . . . Pleads for advice on the "Negroes" . . . CSA expropriates the salt works . . . Discussion of options for idle slaves . . . Isolation.

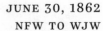

June the 30/62
At Home

Dear Husband

I again seat myself to write to you although it has not been very long since I wrote to you. This is the fourth letter I have written to you since you left home. There has [been] only two months & a few days elapsed since you left home but to look back upon the time it appears fully double that length of time. This leaves us all well at present. I have just returned from Pa, got home yesterday. They were all well there. George Birdwell's oldest child died last Thursday. Mr. Lawler lost his two youngest children. They died with the sore throat [diphtheria?] which is prevailing among the children. The doctors have some technical name for it but I do not know what it is suffice it to say it is very fatal. The health of the country is tolerably good though there has been a good many more deaths this year so far than there were last. The most of the sickness this year is of a very malignant form & very hard to break up though we have escaped so far. I am in daily dread. They have the measels at Henry's. We are now suffering immensely for rain. The corn is in the twist [early corn problem from drought] a greater portion of the day. If we do not get rain before long we will be a ruined people. I want you to write to me what to do about farming as I think Martin undoubtedly will have to leave. Pa says he will be sure to have to go. If he does what must I do? Pa says he thinks that the best plan would be to get a cropper [sharecropper] then we would have to build a house. If I cannot get some person to live with one of us, would it not be a good idea to hire Marshall, Tom, Jess & Charles out next year. We could not get money for them I know but we could get corn & that would be all they could make at home. They would not do that without some person to coerce them and would be a dead expense on my hands. I am willing to try to do anything that you want me to do but I could not do much in that line you know. Pa did not start to the salt Saline as he expected, having heard that there was not salt there. The government has pressed the Saline until they get enough for the army. Our folks [slaves] are not doing much of anything since they laid the crops by. They have not been at anything of any profit for two weeks but Martin says that he is going to put them to work next week. I do not think that he intends to work with them any longer this year. He will commence again at planting time if he does not have to go off to the war. He will instruct them about what to do. I had rather have some person to live with me if I try to make a crop. Pa spoke of that kinsman of his that came out last winter. He has made a crop with old Mr. Nobles who lives in Kaufman.[1] He thinks that he will just fill the bill & is over age under the Conscript law. I guess you recollect about his coming around last winter. His name is James Watkins. What do you think of the arrangement? There has been nothing said about it to him as yet. Pa & me talked about it between us. I have Freedom [WJW's horse] at my house yet & will keep him until fall when Pa intends to sell him. I had rather that you would pay him for Scott so I could get him back. If you can do so I would be very glad. I will be entirely alone if he is sold. If you are willing I had rather the Negroes were hired out than to keep them home. If I could hire them to some person that would treat them well I would prefer it. Jim & Newton Ensley, Burrel Thomas, Thomas Mosely & William Lee have enlisted. Martin still sticks out and will not enlist. The enrolling officer is on his rounds now & Pa says that he will have to go. John Whitfield started for Tyler today [to enlist]. All of the fragments of the different regts are ordered there to form a regiment with the privilege of rejoining their own when the opportunity offers. I am alone except Sallie [female slave] & have been since you left as at least the greater portion of the time.

So write every week to your most devoted wife.
NF Whatley

[Left margin] Jack Walker got home last week from Ark. He is sick.

1. Kaufman is the seat of Kaufman County, 110 miles west of Henderson.

JULY 1862

"Tell the Negroes to attend to business and stay at
home and mind what they are told."

*In high spirits . . . Gave the Feds "a fright" . . . A river war . . . 4th of July cel-
ebration . . . "A perfect terror to the feds" . . . Commentary on Arkansas River
country . . . Unionists . . . Lots of advice: send the boys to school, childrearing,
Negroes.*

July 6th, 1862
West Point, Arkansas

My Dear Wife

As you requested me in your letter to write to you often, I have
seated myself tonight with my saddle in my lap to comply with that
request. I have but little to write that will interest you but know you
want to hear from me. My health is better than it has been at any
time since I left home, am able to eat all I can get and sometimes
more. I have been on a hard scout party for six days which has reduced our horses somewhat but we are now getting some corn. The
feds have been scattered all along the White river from Batesville
down to this place and in fact below but since we came here and

have charged them a few times they have taken a fright and are going down the river and trying to get to their gun boats. Our scout of about one hundred and thirty men celebrated the 4th of July by firing on them in their flatboats going down the river killing I suppose about thirty. They had cotton piled up around them and screened them from our fire. The remainder of our regiment and brigade are now at Duval's [DeValls Bluff] Bluff on White River about thirty miles below here and I suppose are cropping the river to take a stand where we aim to stop them and cut them off from their gun boats. We will start down there to Mason and join our regiment so you may see that we expect to show our plan soon. I think we will have about a thousand men and about forty pieces of cannon (so I hear). Since I last wrote to you I have passed through the most of the fed camp where they have camped all over this country. They have made great destruction in this country taking every thing that the people had to live upon and Negroes and a great many other things that they had no use for but just took them and destroyed them. I find the secessionists in this country to be as clever folks as I ever saw. They will divide the last mouthful with the soldier and more especially with a Texas ranger (as they call us) for they have a great deal more confidence in us than they have in their own troops, and I assure you that we are a perfect terror to the feds. May I never disgrace the name. The health of our soldiers is improving. My mess John Colley, Dick Sanders and Patrick are all in fine health. Dick says you must give his best respects to Miss Dinisha Barkham and cousin Hardin's girls and says he don't think he will marry in Ark but I think if the war should close any time soon that he would not return single. I have not seen Mr. Miller or the other boys in five or six days as we have been off from the main command in a scouting party but will return soon to our regiment. They were all well when I saw them last. This place is the head of navigation on Little Red river and about fifteen miles above where it empties into the White river. I have seen some very fine country here and some poor. The water is generally good. I think better than Texas. On an average it is a better grain country. The wheat here is tolerable good that which was not destroyed by the feds and they make from forty to fifty bushels of corn to the acre but there are so many union men here that I don't think it would suit me to live among them.[1] I do believe some of them are worse than the feds, they have gone and pointed out the Sesesh (as they call us) and their provisions to the feds and been the cause of their getting a great many things that they otherwise would not have got, and since we have come up here they have taken a fright and a good many have run over and joined the federal army. We have arrested a good many of them and when we had proof imprisoned them and turned all the young ones into the army. I am getting anxious to hear from you again as I have not had but one letter from you, but must think you have wrote. You must write to me upon the receipt of all my letters if not oftener as your chance is better than mine. I do hope you will all keep well and get along well for my Dear wife I assure that your condition will not compare with the conditions of a great many here. I was pleased to learn in your letter that you were getting along better than you had expected. I hope you will be of good cheer and bear our separation with fortitude. Take good care of the children and learn them to mind. You must control them but mind that you do it with affection, and if you have any chance send the boys to school and let them be learning. Our mail is still at Little Rock. It is brought from there up by an express. So you will continue to direct to that point Taylor's Regiment Company F. When you write give me all the news about the place, how your crop is and so on. My horse has gone down considerable but it is impossible to keep a horse up under the heavy scouting that we have to do, when it is impossible to get corn all the time. You must remember me to all the kin. I expect I will get a letter from you when I get back to the regiment and if I do I will answer it the first opportunity. Tell the children they must not forget their pa. They must be good children and mind you and when I come home I will bring them something nice. I have already written to you about the death of our Captain. It was a great misfortune to our company. Write soon and give me all the news. Tell the Negroes to attend to business and stay at home and mind what they are told. I will now close by subscribing myself

Your Husband in love
WJ Whatley

1. William's axis of travel to the Little Rock and Arkansas River region touched on the southern edge of northwest Arkansas Unionism, an area of ferocious guerrilla warfare with raiding back and forth from Missouri.

JULY 13, 1862
WJW TO NFW

"The prevailing opinion is that Gen[eral] Rust was drunk."

WJW appetite and health . . . Description of major battle . . . General Rust . . . Texans are down on Arkansas commanders . . . Dismounted and forage issues . . . A plundered country.

July 13th 1862
Camp near Brownsville

Dearest object of my love.

I have this day received two letters from you which afforded me a great deal of pleasure. Was very glad to hear you were all well and doing well, but fear from the way you wrote in your last letter (of the 20th) that you will have a drought that will cut off the crop but hope however that you will make a plenty and have your health and enjoy it the best you can in my absence. As for me I am in as good health as I ever enjoyed in my life and have a good appetite. Can eat a pone of bread and two or three rations of bacon any morning for breakfast with a good relish. We had an engagement last Monday with Gen. Curtis's [Union commander and victor at Pea Ridge] army near cotton plant [Cotton Plant, Woodruff County, site of Battle of Hill's Plantation one week before] about ten miles east of Des Ark

[Arc] on White River in which there was Col. Parsons Regiment, Col Fitzhue [Fitzhugh], Taylor's company is a part of Sucet's. I was not there having been sent on detached service about a week before. I will give you the account as I learned it from those who were in the fight. It is thought that the feds had about ten thousand men and several batteries of artillery which played havoc with our men. Col. Parsons was ordered on to make the attack and we lost about one hundred of his men in killed and wounded. Col Fitzhugh lost about twenty and was wounded in two or three places himself. There was only about a hundred of Col Sucets men who were ordered to dismount and form a line which they did and waited until the feds were in thirty or forty yards of them before they knew them from our men as they were dressed like us and the commander ordered them to surrender and stack their arms. They replied by shooting him and fired on them and then had to retreat to their horses but they killed a many a fed before they left. Our regiment was ordered to their rear to cut off their retreat and had to run their horses about fifteen miles to get there and then met such a strong force that they had to retreat. The prevailing opinion is that Gen Rust was drunk and led his men into a trap. I think the fight was about a stand off and we did not have more than two thousand men engaged about five to one. The Texans are all down on the Arkansas commanders. We are now dismounted, our horses run down and it is impossible for us to ride them much longer. They will be sent home soon. The men grumble a good deal about being dismounted but will consent as it is impossible to get forage. I think I will be one of the detail to bring them home and will probably see you before this reaches you but have concluded to write any how to answer your letter. I will say to you that this country has [been] run over and the good all taken by the feds. There is not a yard of cloth in this country nor a plug of tobacco nor paper nor in fact anything else but if I come home I will bring you a dress if I can find anything to make it of or will send it to you if I can and don't come myself. Your brother Jess[e] has passed through Little Rock on his way home, him and Aaron afoot. Mr. Miller will be home soon. Jack Easley is dead, died at Brownsville [Arkansas] two or three days ago. Some of the other boys sick but nothing serious. There will be five or six men detailed out of our company but don't know whether any of them will be sent or not. I will close as there is such a bustle here that I am confused. The health here is better.

I remain your affectionate Husband.
WJ Whatley

"I want you to write to me something about . . . next year
with regard to farming arrangements."

Good news about brother Jesse . . . Drought continues . . . Corn crop failure . . . Isolation, someone to stay with her . . . Anxiety about the "present arrangement"—What to do with the "Negroes" . . . Martin eludes conscription.

At Home, July the 19th/62

My dearest husband,

I seat myself this lovely morning to drop you a few lines that you may know how we are getting along. This leaves us all up on foot. My own health is about the same I think. I am never well but manage to keep up pretty much all the time. I will try to be satisfied if I can only be up at least as well contented as I can be while separated from you. I have some good news for you. Brother Jesse has got home [from Memphis]. He returned last Tuesday. They made the trip on foot all the way except four days uncle gave him a very fine saddle animal & an old mule that would have made the trip very well but they were told that they could not possibly cross the river with them and he sent them back to uncle but when they got to the river they could have been gotten over easy. Uncle gave him $180 to buy him a horse with when he crossed the river but he could not get it for love nor money for a week & he thought that as he had to walk that far he would not try to get one for the balance of the trip. He passed a camp on the morning of the fourth of this month that he was told was the place that Taylor's regiment camped the night before on their way to Duvall's [DeValls] Bluff to prevent the landing of troops by the enemy. I am getting anxious to hear from you again. We are still suffering very much for rain having none in ten weeks except little sprinkles which did more harm than good. My corn is not near as good as we thought it was. Since it began to get hard it has shriveled up there was good as we thought good ears it has turned out to be nary more shuck than corn. The piece of new ground the other side of the orchard is very good but the upland is sorry. The old bottom is not good. The young corn in the new ground would make tolerable good corn if it would rain immediately but not near as good as it would have been with rain in due time. I let cousin Syl have your rifle for James.[1] I did not know whether I was doing right or not but under the circumstances of the case I could not well do otherwise. Pa was down to see me this week. He came down Friday & went back next day. He has never got the letter you wrote to him yet has sent for it once. He thinks that it may be that the man is sick. If not there is some rascality about it. I want you to write to me something about what I had best do next year with regard to farming arrangements. I had rather have somebody to live with me as I think that it would result in ultimate benefit to us. It would take a great deal off me that I now have to see to as I am but poorly able to see to it. Pa says that would be much the best for me. From the way things are going on now our Negroes will not be of any permanent benefit to us until Martin gets ready to fix for planting as he is not taking much interest in what they are doing. He comes over occasionally and gives them some instructions about their work. He has just got home been gone all the week to the muster [Nacogdoches]. He was gone the most of the week before. Our folks have been pulling fodder for a week. It is burnt up & the corn is not ripe enough yet, only in spots. Consequently they are pulling in spots. Pa thinks that it would be the best arrangement to get some one to live with me even if Mr. Martin does not go to the war as they could see to things about the place for me which I am necessarily bound to see after now with the present arrangements. Pa thinks that a cousin of ours, James Watkins, would be the best chance for me if the plan meets with your approbation. He made a crop with old Mr. Nobles this year & from the recommendation that uncle Dick [Richard Overton Watkins (1816–1897), brother of A. H. Watkins] gives him he will be the man for me. He had conditionally hired him himself but under the circumstances by which I am surrounded he would give way to me but that was all that would induce him to give him up. Pa wrote to him before Martin got to be over the conscript law thinking he was still 32. Write often and lengthy.

Your loving wife, NF Whatley

1. This individual is not identified. He is not the same James as the cousin (James Watkins) mentioned later in this letter.

AUGUST 1862

No letters survive from August 1862. In a July letter, WJW mentioned detached service and that he might be returning to Texas with the regiment's horses. He did return to Caledonia, then went to Henderson, from there to Gilmer, then Sulphur, and on into Arkansas via Arkadelphia to Camp Hope (later Camp Nelson), thirty miles northeast of Little Rock. There, in mid-September, he rejoined the Seventeenth.

SEPTEMBER 1862

"Have been pretty sore walking. I sent my horse back."

Returning to Arkansas after delivering horses . . . No marbles for the boys . . . Save his tack for future remounting.

> Camp 13 miles above
> Sulphur Bowie County
> Texas Sept 6th 1862

Dear wife

I drop you a line this evening to let you know how I am getting along as I know you will be getting anxious by this time to hear from me. Well after I left you I went to your fathers and stayed all night. Jesse did not go with me agreeable to [his] promise, owing to inability. So I went on safe to Gilmer [sixty miles north of Caledonia] by the 1st of this month and started on our line of march the 2nd and have traveled about fifteen miles per day. I find walking pretty laborious. The weather is quite warm, but have had fine rain which helps the cause very much. We are now in about thirty five miles of Fulton [Arkansas, 10 miles northwest of Texarkana] on Red River and have stoped to day at twelve oclock to rest till morning when we will again set out and if we have good luck will get to our regiment about the 18th. It is nice at Austin about twenty five miles beyond Little Rock. We have come through Dangerfield in Titus county and Davis Waterhouses regiment is halted at Rondo [Arkansas] about twenty miles from here on our road and I suppose will remain there some time.[1] I shall go to see the boys in Wallaces Company when I get there. My health has been very good since I left but have been pretty sore walking. I sent my horse back by Jo Becton who promised me he would take him to [unreadable], who will keep him until he can be sent for. I must [stop] soon as the gentleman is now waiting to take this to Marshal [Texas] to mail for me. Tell the boys that I had no chance to send them any marbles but will the first chance. You must do the best you can and take care of the children. If the conscript law is raised and Mr. Martin has to go you must do the best you can and if you can't get the right [help] of a man over fifty you had best have more. You can write to me at Little Rock if you have not done so as soon as you receive this and give me all the news. Tell me all about the affairs at home and how you are getting along. Take care of my horse, saddle, bridle, saddle bags, & so if I am mounted I can have them.

    Your Husband
    W. J. Whatley

1. William wrote the wrong first name for Colonel Richard Waterhouse, a merchant of Jefferson, Texas. Waterhouse was commissioned in 1862 to raise a regiment, the Nineteenth Texas, from the northeast Texas counties, which was later absorbed into Walker's brigade.

SEPTEMBER 13, 1862
WJW TO NFW

"I often think of you and my little children who I have left behind in your lonely desolated condition . . . when I again return to you that we will be free and independent and remain together."

Most of the regiment dismounted . . . New preacher . . . Rumors about Beaure-
gard, ironclads, and liberating New Orleans; McClellan and Pope wounded
at Second Bull Run . . . Paper shortages . . . Many questions about the farm
operations . . . On the way to Little Rock.

Arkadelphia, Arkansas
Sept 13th 1862

Dear wife,

As I have another opportunity I avail myself of it to drop you a
few lines that you may hear from me. I have just arrived here well
and hearty and am getting so that walking can't hurt me. We have
traveled about fifteen miles per day and some days more. Have had
plenty of rain and got along pleasantly. We have now about thirty
men and about five of them are riding which gives me an occasional
chance to ride. We have a preacher with us who belongs to Roberts' regiment [Eleventh Texas Infantry, another East Texas unit]
who has preached for us several times. Since we started, I came by
Rondo [Arkansas] and saw a great many of my acquaintances in
Waterhouse's regiment [Nineteenth Texas Infantry]. The regiment
had stopped there and had a good many sick but none from our
county were much sick with the exception of John Cornel. He was
expected to die the day I was there. At Gilmer [forty miles north of
Henderson], I went to see Mr. Looney open his school & hear him
lecture.[1] I am very much pleased with him. I think he is an excellent
teacher, and fully understands his business. We have lately had some
very good news, if true. I read a dispatch yesterday which [stated]
that General Beauregard had just returned from France with fifteen
ironclad vessels and had retaken New Orleans and all & that we had
taken several places in Kentucky. It is also stated that Generals Mc-
Clellan & Pope are both wounded and a huge portion of their arms
taken.[2] So it seems that our armies have achieved several victories
in the last few weeks. It is reported that our army will start for Missouri by the sixteenth of this month, but I don't think it is so. I have

ordered you a paper that is published in our camps which will keep you posted as to the movement of the army and will give you more news than I can write. You must be very saving with your writing paper for when that is gone I fear you will not be able to get any more. I have tried all the ways to buy and can't find a sheet. You must write me how many turnips you have sowed and all about your affairs. Write me how much corn you have cribbed. I think you will have plenty of mast [acorn crop] to fatten your hogs. You must take care of your corn, and let the mules run in the pasture. You had better sow what barley you have and get a bushel or two of rye and sow for a winter pasture. Cousin Syl is to let me have two bushels of wheat, one of white wheat and one of red. I told Mr. Martin where to sow it. The mail will leave here soon and as I want to get this in I shall have to cut it short. We are now about seventy five miles from Little Rock and about a hundred from our regiment and will get there in six or seven days from this time. I often think of you and my little children who I have left behind in your lonely desolated condition but try to console myself with the hope that when I again return to you that we will be free and independent and can remain together. Tell the children they must love their pa while he's gone and be good children and mind what you tell them. You must encourage the Negroes and tell them they must do their best. My best respects to Mr. Martin and family, Mr. Miller & family and in fact to all friends and relations, and believe that this is from your ever true and devoted Husband.

WJ Whatley

1. WJW was interested in education and left in the family papers a brief treatise on the importance of education. See Doyal T. Loyd, "Morgan H. Looney and His Gilmer School, 1861–1871," *East Texas Historical Journal* 15.1 (1977): 20–23. Available at http://scholarworks.sfasu.edu/ethj/vol15/iss1/7.

2. The Confederacy was on the edge of taking Kentucky out of the war and capturing the great prize of Cincinnati. The campaign to seize Cincinnati collapsed and most of the Confederate gains were lost as Bragg and others pulled back into Tennessee, southeast of Nashville, for the winter. Second Manassas/Bull Run was a tactical victory for the Confederacy.

"Do please write to me what to do for I am very much disturbed in mind."

Farm news . . . Martin prepares for service . . . NFW desperate about her mounting responsibilities . . . The men have all concluded that they will have to go . . . Pleads for advice.

September 14th/62
At Home

To My Husband

I seat myself to drop you a few lines that you may know how we are getting along. We are in good health except one of the children was complaining this evening but it is nothing. [He or she] was perfectly well yesterday. I think that it is an attack of colic. I got the letter that you mailed from Gilmer he sent it to me last . . . come down & spent two days with me. I have not got your horse home yet but he is . . . I will send for him tomorrow & he shall have every attention that is necessary to make him fat. I think that when you send for him that I shall start him to you with all the flesh that he will take on that is if it is long enough for him to get fat before you send for him. We got rain enough to sow turnips last Thursday night but have sowed none yet. Martin put Jess [slave] to breaking up the ground & and he has not done two days work at it in a week. Martin is at work at his well yet has not got it fixed yet but will finish some time this week. They finished hauling up that corn they [laid] down the last of week before last. They had fourteen good loads in that field. I think that there is five hundred bushels now in the crib. The cotton has been hauled to the gin. We had eight big loads or as much as that body will hold. Tom [slave] is not able to work yet but I think will be in a few days. Mr. Martin is fixing for the war or at least has now concluded that he will have to go & is fixing up at home as well as he can before he has to leave. I do not know what to do. It looks like it will be a breaking up business for me to leave home but if I stay here & make nothing not even a support that will not do. Pa says that it will never do for me to stay at home & no one with me to see to do anything for me. I have thought that if I did have to leave home which I will not do as long as there is any other chance for me to get along that if I could get Mr. Miller to take Marshal & let me furnish his provisions & mule & get him to take the oversight of the place & keep the fence up so the stock will not destroy everything. Believe me that I cannot leave home without making arrangements so that [Marshal] will not leave it to be destroyed. It will be at a sacrifice that . . . any arrangements that can be made . . . not be as much as the loss of a . . . I know if I had any judgment about . . . will be another thing but as it is . . . neither have any judgment & where that will take control there will be . . . but I do not want you to understand that I am anxious to leave home for such is not the case unless I am obliged to leave. I will not go & if I do have to leave it will be at the latest moment. You must write to me what you want me to do & I will endeavor to come as nigh it as I can possibly do. I do not want you to pass it by without giving me a positive answer about what you want me to do. Look at it in all its bearings & the consequences of my going & also what the consequences of staying at home & failing to make a crop will be. The greatest loss that I apprehend if I go away will be in hogs and sheep for I cannot take them with me. Any reasons for thinking that if I go I had best leave Marshal to take care of the hogs & feed them? I want you to write to me what is best to do for the men have all concluded that they will have to go & it is of no use to try to evade it any longer. Do please write to me what to do for I am very much disturbed in mind. I expect that you will think that because I have seen Ma I am worse than I could have been if I had not seen her but I was worse before I saw her than I am now. The doctors have given Mrs. Johnson out to die, also George Roads, Drew Staten is very sick. Indeed I would not be surprised that she died Monday morning. Marshal is some better this morning. I am going to send for Freedom [WJW's horse] this morning. You must write to me often, very often. I will send this up to Pa's & have it mailed. Do please write often. The children often speak of you.

From your affectionate wife,
N. F. Whatley

"We must defend our rights. . . . I don't think this war
can last more than six months."

Letter and money on the way . . . Pay his debt to Mr. Miller . . . Preparing to move . . . Signs of winter . . . Dependent upon Mr. Martin . . . If he gets drafted she has to move . . . What to do with the slaves . . . Five hours of daily drill . . . No furloughs . . . Lots of beef . . . Rigorous discipline . . . Instructions on caring for the hogs.

Camp Hope Arkansas[1]
September 20th 1862

My Dear Wife,

Yours of the 14th of this month has just come to hand and it is with much pleasure that I hasten to reply. Was very glad to know that you were all well and hope you will continue so for nothing on earth now affords me half so much pleasure as to hear from my family and to hear that they are in good health. I am happy to communicate to you that I am enjoying the same great blessing. I have no news of importance to write to you. I have been here now a week tomorrow and have resumed my duties as a soldier and getting along very well. There are a great many troops here and but little sickness considering the no [number] of men, I wrote to you a few days since by

Isaac Morris and sent in the letter by him three hundred and eighty dollars. He promises me that he would take the money to you. There are full instructions in the letter about it which you will understand and pay over to Mr. Miller his part which is all but a hundred. It is rumored here today that the wagons have all been ordered in from the wagon yard to be here Monday morning preparatory to starting from here to some other point, but there is no telling about when we will leave, as the most of the regiments are just now sending home for clothing and it is believed that we will remain here until we get them. We are now having some quite cool nights and mornings which begins to warn us of the approach of winter which I fear will go pretty hard with us in a northern climate. You write that Mr. Martin is fixing to leave for the army. I had hoped and still hope that he will not be forced to go but if he does it cannot be helped and will leave you in a bad fix and I don't know hardly how to advise you. I have studied the matter over since last night and must confess that I am still at a loss about what you had best do. It does seem to me that it will be mighty bad to break up and leave home, and let the stock scatter and the place go to rack. Indeed it will be but little better than a burning, and to leave the Negroes there by themselves will be mighty bad. I fear they will not do anything and perhaps get into trouble, but if the people have to leave up to forty five [Conscription Act of 1862] I cannot be satisfied for you to remain by yourself. I am not fully advised of your notions of moving, (you would go to your fathers of course) but do you think you can stay there contented, and would you move the Negroes and stock and other plunder, or only the white family and household, and if the Negroes, would your Pa have land for them to work. These are matters that bother me considerably. I will just say to you as you have enjoined it on me to do say that you had better stay at home, until you know that Martin is compelled to go (perhaps he may yet get out) and then if it is possible to get any one that will do to depend on you had better get him at any cost than to leave home. But if Martin leaves and you cannot get anyone else, I don't think it will do for you to stay at home alone. You can go to your Pa's or keep house yourself if you can get the Birdwell houses, and move up such things as you will need and leave the balance at home to be taken care of by who ever you leave.[2] Your notions are very good about that, it will never do to give up home entirely. If you can make such an arrangement with Mr. Miller as you speak of perhaps it will be best, and if your Pa has not got land enough for your force [their slaves] and his to cultivate without paying rent you had better leave our force at home (or at Mr. Miller's if he will see that they do anything). I would greatly prefer selling to breaking up and leaving if it could be done. I would rather let old man Jones have it back at a sacrifice if he would take it, but I reckon there will be no chance for that. I want you however to stay at home a while until we can see a little farther into the war for it is not at all improbable that we will have peace by next spring, and if such was the case a move would be very much against us. You now have my notions in full about the matter, and have still not told you positively what to do, from the fact that I am unable to do so, but want you to consult with your pa and do what you think is for the best. I hope you understand me. In the first place stay until Martin leaves, and next get someone else if you can and as the last resort leave home and make the best arrangement you can. We are now drilling about five hours a day which is pretty good exercise. My walk just put me in fine plight for the drill. We have only about thirty men that are on duty besides sick, details, and furloughed men. The general has now stopped furloughs for the present, but I reckon they will be granted again soon if we don't take up the line of march. We are now drawing meal plenty and a pound and a quarter of beef per day which does us very well. Some of the boys grumble because they don't get bacon but for my part I am very well satisfied with beef. I think they are trying to get all the bacon they can to travel on when they leave here. We have a beautiful location here [Camp Hope] and plenty of good water and I hope we will remain here until we take up the line of march for parts unknown. We are now on pretty tight duty but I think it is best for health and that suits me. Everything that a soldier needs here is out of all reason. You cannot buy anything in Little Rock without paying four, five to ten prices, and as we are now dismounted we have no chance to go anywhere: keep out a regular camp & picket guard day and night, and we are forbid to go out of camp for any purpose whatever without permission from an officer. There is pretty strict discipline but I don't think it is any too strict for it don't hurt honest men and makes others do their duty. I don't much think now that we will be remounted, and I don't think it will be necessary for you to take any very extra pains with Freedom. Let him run in the pasture and keep him in good order and if I find that [I] shall need him at any time I will let you know. When you get the corn all gathered if you have it to spare let Mrs. Russel have enough to pay what [we] owe Thad at a dollar per bushel if she wants it but you must be sure to keep enough for your use. Write me if there is mast enough to fatten the hogs.[3] I was under the impression when I left home that there would be a plenty of white oak [for acorns] which with the peas would fatten your pigs. You must have plenty of peas saved for seed, and have as much improvements done as you can about the place and fix the fences all up. Tell Mr. Miller that Capt Brewton [Captain Joseph H. Bruton, Company H] has drawed Mr. Statons money, but can't pay it over without legal steps are taken which say here is a regular administration. Gustavus Treadwell has paid the balance on his notes and taken them up (625) which I will send the first good chance. I think we will draw again about the 1st of next month and I will then make a heavy effort for him and get all I can. Write me how Colby is getting on, and be sure to send me a little tobacco the first chance you have. You must have the hogs attended to and keep the pigs marked that you may not loose them. I feel for you and the children in your lonely condition, but it is unavoidable. We must defend our rights but I hope the time is drawing nigh when we will be together again for I don't think this war can last more than six months. Tell little Jane I will nurse her and sweetly then, tell them to be good children and kiss them all for me. Give my love to all the kin. I would be glad to hear from any of them. You must be sure to write on the receipt of this and let me know all about your affairs. I will write to you when I can, but have but little time. I have been part of two days at this, just a few lines at a time. I send you in this my tax rect which you will file away.

Your affectionate Husband,
W. J. Whatley

1. Camp Hope (later Camp Nelson), northeast of Little Rock, was a death trap of disease as well as the site of an 1862 mutiny with nine enlisted men executed. In 1861–1862, up to 20,000 Arkansas and Texas troops were based there, mostly inactive, and suffered huge losses from disease and dysentery.

2. "Birdwell houses": Birdwells were scattered throughout the southern part of Rusk County. John C. Birdwell left a collection of letters, now at Stephen F. Austin University, Nacogdoches, Texas, which bitterly criticized the twenty-slave exemption provision in the Conscription Act of 1862 and protested having to fight a "rich man's war." He also served in Taylor's Seventeenth Cavalry (Dismounted), was at the Battle of Mansfield, died about the same time as William, and was buried at Pine Grove Cemetery.

3. Peter Wohlleben, *The Hidden Life of Trees*, trans. Jane Billinghurst (Vancouver: Greystone Books, 2015). "Mast year" refers to the year when oaks set an unusual amount of seed and the acorn yield is tremendous. Farmers like William would herd their hogs into the oak groves and the beasts would gorge on the acorns and fatten on nature's bounty.

SEPTEMBER 21, 1862
WJW TO NFW

"We have a good deal of news afloat here but don't know
how to separate the chaff from the wheat."

News of Rusk County men . . . Optimistic rumors of Confederate victories and Lincoln proposing peace . . . Coincides with the Battle of Antietam . . . Informs her about pay, debts, notes, and complicated debt relationships and what to do with the money . . . Send tobacco . . . Needs clothes . . . Admonishes NFW to save her paper.

Camp Hope, 6 miles from Austin
September 21st 1862

It is 380.00. I send 100.00 for you. 240.00 for Mr. Miller. [WJW sent NJW money.]

My Dear Wife,

This will inform you that I have arrived safe in camp. I got here yesterday after a journey of three weeks and in my usual good health. [Note: WJW had been in camp for about a week and didn't appear to be interested in accuracy here.] I find quite an army here and some sickness but not many dangerous cases. There has been several deaths in our regiment since I left but no one in our company. I find Patrick sick but up and about. Dick Sanders is well. Thad, James Mosely, Treadwell, and Evans & Hillers are well. Al Thomas is sick and Slaturn is dead. We have a good deal of news afloat here but don't know how to separate the chaff from the wheat. We have news that General Kirby Smith had taken Cincinnati on the 8th and also that Stonewall Jackson was marching on Baltimore and that the federals were evacuating Washington City [the Union stopped Lee at Antietam, September 17, 1862] and a good many more important movements, among which is that Lincoln had made propositions for peace. I am unable to say how much of this true but I am satisfied that we are wearing them badly at this time. We had a complete victory at Manassas [Second Bull Run] routing their army. Our camp paper has been stopped, by order of Gen Holmes, and in consequence thereof I have sent you the Little Rock True Democrat, which will give you all the war news that is afloat in this section of country. Our army is now being furnished with arms. Some regiments have been armed entirely and two companies of ours. I do not know when we will leave here or where we will go. While writing my ears are pierced with the sound of musket and drum paying the last sad tribute to a departed soldier and burying him with military honor and hear others whistling and singing at the same time. Alas how hard is the human heart. I have saved my wages of 125.00 and will draw my bounty down.[1] It is ready for me any time I see the quartermaster. I will send you a hundred dollars in this letter by Isaac Morris who is here now and will shortly leave in a day or two. He had come up to see after the effects of his son who died not long since. You can pay the money over to your father if he wants it, as we owe him or keep it and use if you need it. I expect we will draw again soon, and I will have plenty for my own uses. I want you to tell Mr. Martin to put me up some tobacco and you send me a little by Colby when he comes if he will bring it and by any other opportunities you may have. I don't want but little at a time as I can't take care of it. If you have an opportunity send me my other jeans coat as the one I have don't suit me, too small to wear over my over shirt. Jimmy Walker is here, got here about two days before me and is well. I met Jack about thirty miles beyond Little Rock going back to go to his own regiment. He had been up to get a transfer to join [his] regiment but could not succeed. Tell Mr. Miller that I will send him what money I can get for him soon. I have seen some of the boys they talk like they will pay some money. Thad has payed his horse note to Weatherly and Evans has payed his, Hillers has paid Olds 17.50, so this has all been paid to Weatherly and sent home by L.L. Murphy except about five dollars which he will pay to me when we can get change. I think I can get the fellows that Thad owes and enough from Hillers to take up one note. I have not talked to any of the other boys yet as they are out today in other regiments. Al Thomas has sent his money home Thad tells me, but says the others he thinks has theirs. I will be unable to do anything with the Slaturn [recently deceased] note now. Capt Brewton has the money but I suppose they can't pay it out without the estate is administered on. I will do the best I can for him. I have had no letter from you and am anxious to hear from home. This is the third letter I have written. Tell your pa I mailed his letter at Little Rock according to promise. You must save your paper as it is almost impossible to get any more and to be debared the pleasure of hearing from you and the children would almost unnerve me. I often think of you and my dear children and hope this time will speedily come when we will be together again and enjoy peace and harmony around our own fireside. Tell them to be good boys and girls and when I come home I will bring them something pretty. The Negroes must go ahead with business and make a big crop next year. I have seen the boys got what money I can from them which is as follows. From B.F. Treadwell fifty five dollars, from Gustavus a hundred and five, from Thad forty and from Hillers eighty, forty of which he wants Mr. Miller to pay over to his mother. I have only credited his notes with forty. I find three hundred dollars, one hundred for you, two hundred for Mr. Miller and the forty that Hillers wants his mother to have. I think we will draw again in about ten days and the boys say they will pay more then and will send more in about ten days when I have a good chance.

> My love to all and remember your husband
> W. J. Whatley

1. Another reason that WJW did not return home was this would risk forfeiting his enlistment bounty.

SEPTEMBER 22, 1862

NFW TO WJW

"I am troubled more than ever."

Martin's indifferent, vexing mismanagement . . . Water well collapse . . . NFW attended preaching . . . Description of a camp meeting . . . Funeral planned for her brother James . . . Local wedding and visit of sister Jane . . . Rumor of slave conscription . . . Isolation . . . Corn crop and saving the hogs . . . Health news.

Sept the 22nd At Home

Rusk Cty Texas

Dearest Husband,

I seat myself this evening to answer your letter which I received four days ago & would have written to you sooner but I wrote to [you] about three days before I received yours. This leaves us all up again. Jess has been quite sick with fever, but it is now broke on him and he is now out of danger. Marshal has been sick also but he laid up only three days. Sam [slave] went to work this morning. It is the first steady work that he has done. They are pulling down Martin's corn now. They have only hauled up the corn they had down when you left & sowed turnips. They have not even fenced them in yet. The cotton has been hauled to the gin. That is all the work that they have done since you left. It is the worst management that I ever saw in my life. My well is out of repair & it looks like it is impossible for me to get Martin to fix it. I intend to send to Pa's & see if I cannot get him to have it fixed for me as it is dangerous to draw water there now. The entire curbing is decayed & it is with the best of care that we can even get a bucket of water now & there is no other that we could use if it was to fall in which it is liable to do at any moment. One half has gone down nearly a foot lower than the other sides. It is very dangerous for we cannot close it off at all. I have been to preaching for the last two days at Shiloh [Rusk County hamlet near Caledonia]. The association met there. We had sermon in the morning from Elder Rowland & in the evening from Rogers.[1] This morning we had prayer meeting and exhortation which was lengthened out to a sermon before he quit. They are still protracting the meeting. There was some ten or twelve mourners today.[2] Among the rest was Lil, Tresia, and Mary Walker. There is a Methodist meeting going on at Caledonia. They have had a general stir up there so I hear, several sessions. I am going up to Pa's this week. They will send for me as they have concluded to have James [James Watkins (1841–1862) and NFW's brother] funeral sermon preached. Parson Slayter will preach it. I will go hear it preached & will go probably from there to Aunt Mary's as she sent me word that she would be there that day. There is a good many cases of fever & more chills than there has been this year. Mrs. Johnson has been sick ever since before you left. She will die I guess. She is reduced to skin and bones. Jack Walker wrote back that it was all a mistake about his being published to the world as a deserter, that there was no such talk, only at his uncle's & he was drinking when he said it that they all thought that he was dead. There has been a wedding lately, Ben Jones and Bettie Fields. They married last Sunday morning. Jane [Watkins] come down last Monday for a week & staid until Saturday morning when she went home to the wedding. There is a law now in force so I hear to take all of the Negroes over 20 and under 30 which will take Aaron & George both & will leave Pa in a bad fix to make corn.[3] It seems to me that I am troubled more than ever for I cannot see how I will make a living. I do not know anything about farming or management & the Negroes do not take any control at all, only when they are made & I am confident that I will have to feed them & they will not support themselves which will not pay. I am trying to get things fixed up about the place the best that I can but Martin is as contrary as he possibly can be. He puts the Negroes at one thing one day & at another the next & the consequence is that they do nothing at all but when they go to work at his house they keep going. He is going to see to your business until all the hauling gets done & then he does not know what he will do so I hear from others. The way he is doing now I can a do great deal better without him for he has hurt my feelings lately anyhow. He is not willing for me to have a say about anything that you think best about it. Write to me what to do about it. I want you to write to me if you think that you can get a furlough to come home when your first year expires. I never knew what it was to be lonesome before. Jane came down to see me once but staid only two nights & one day I had cousin Syl, cousin Vicey, Jack, Rachel, Mary Sallie to spend the day with me on the fourth, also cousin Lills, Lex, & Miss Hopson. I stay alone nearly all the time but am very lonesome. I do not think that Ma has done me right about Jane staying with me but she says that I might have come up there to stay. She does not think that there is much the matter for me. I read a letter from Mr. Miller written since yours in which he said that you were drawing only half rations which I was very sorry to hear. It is bad enough to be away from home & be well & plenty to eat but it is so much worse when you are sick & not enough to eat & cannot eat what you have. I scarcely ever go to eat but what I think of you & wonder where you are & what you are doing & often wish that I knew whether you had anything or not to eat. If I could only know that you would keep well I could stand almost anything but if I were to hear that you were bad sick & I could not go to you it seems to me it would be more than I could bear but we do not know what we can do until we have the trial. I do hope & pray that you may keep at least in tolerable good health whilst you are gone. I have been over the corn since commencing this letter. I think that we will make about as much with no more rain as we did last year. When I was in the old bottom last I did not think that it would make with the best of seasons any more than it will be sure to make without any more rain now. The corn in that old field is by far the best that we have. If we can get rain the corn will make a big pile. It looks as black as it can well look but without rain it will not make anything, only in spots. We will have an overwhelming mast so the old settlers say & they know. I have not lost one of the hogs this summer but they have gotten very poor. The mules look well. This leaves us all well as usual that is on foot. I have been taking medicine from Dr. Hubbard for a good while. I do not know that there is anything serious the matter but am not right & have not been for twelve months or more that you know. Write often and lengthy.

Your loving wife
N. F. Whatley

1. Itinerant preachers, such as Elder John Rowland, followed the circuit of rural camp meetings and conducted revivals.

2. "Mourners" refers to the camp meeting custom of exhorting participants to come forward to the Mourners' Bench and own up to past sins and repent. Timothy R. Mahoney, *From Hometown to Battlefield in the Civil War Era: Middle Class Life in Midwest America* (New York: Cambridge University Press, 2016), 290.

3. NFW refers to the Confederate Army's practice of impressing slaves for building fortifications and roads as Magruder would do aggressively when he became responsible for Texas's defense.

OCTOBER 1862

"Kiss all the children for me and tell them that I love them . . .
will come home when I kill all the Yankees."

*Vagaries of the mail while on the march . . . Food talk . . . Plenty of beef . . .
Arduous, wet march from Camp Hope . . . Doubts about infantry life . . . Too
much fatigue duty . . . Wants Dr. Watkins to send Jesse [a slave] to serve
him . . . Expecting a fight from Curtis at St. Helena . . . Martin continues to
elude the draft.*

Camp near Clarendon
Arkansas,[1] October 7th /62

My Dear Beloved Wife,

I again snatch a moment to write to you, the greatest of all pleasures
to me. I have been anxiously expecting a letter from you but have not
got but the one yet which responded to soon after its reception, but
I presume you have written and the fault is in the mail. This will be
three letters I have written to you since I got into camp, and three
on the road. You will see by the caption of this that we have moved
since I last wrote to you and that probably accounts for my not get-

ting your precious letters, but the mail will be sent for tomorrow to Little Rock and then I reckon they will come, and if so I will respond again. The health of our army is much better than it has been, in fact we have no sickness in our regiment of a serious nature. My health is as good as ever and am able to eat all I can get and sometimes a little more if I could that would suit me. I often think of the good milk and butter I had at home and wish I could be with you again and sup with you around our own board with two little prattlers on either side. We are drawing beef and bread alone, and since we have been dismounted we have no chance to go out into the country for anything at all and consequently we have no change of diet. Sweet potatoes when they can be had all will sell for three dollars per bushel. In fact we just offered that for some and failed to get them. You must not infer from the above that we are suffering for something to eat for such is not the case. The complaint is not against the quantity so much as quality. We left Camp Hope near Austin on the 1st inst and arrived here on the 4th, a distance of about seventy-five miles the way we traveled and had two days and one night rain on us, which made it very disagreeable traveling, bogging down and stalling our teams and I assure that there was a many of a blistered foot when we landed at this place. Some of the boys give out and didn't get up in a day or two. For my part I suffered no little with head aches but got here with the command. I do not like the infantry service as well as cavalry. We have too much fatigue duty [digging ditches, latrine maintenance, etc.] to perform. We are nearly all the time on duty of some kind which does not agree with my health especially in warm weather, and when we march we generally have to go too far and hard in a country like this where water is scarce and no railroad transportation. Tell your pa that that if he could conclude to send Jesse out here and is willing to send Aaron with him that I will pay him for half his time, and perhaps I can make managements through my mess to pay more than that. I have more duty to perform than I like to do without cooking and washing and the weather here is almost as warm as it was last summer. Our water here is not near so good nor handy as it was at our other camp. Curtis is said to be at

Helena well fortified about sixty miles northwest from here. We are expecting a fight now, soon. All our entire forces have been ordered up here including about thirty regiments of infantry and cavalry and about a hundred pieces of artillery. General Holmes is collecting a great many Negroes they say to fortify over on the river about five miles from here but I don't know hardly what we will do for we only know what we are told to do and that relates alone to our duty and business as soldiers. We have not drawed any more money and I reckon will not draw any more until after we have a fight. I presume from what I hear now that Martin will not have to leave you, but if he does I gave you full instructions in my last about what to do. Tell George Birdwell that I saw William yesterday. He is in good health and says that he has written to him several times. He has got the clothing he sent him by Edgar Hays. I have seen a good many of my acquaintances here in different regiments since I came back. Col. Taylor is now gone home and I think McClarty will go soon which will place Nobles in command, until Taylor gets back and he is expected soon.[2] Give my love to your pa and ma and all the family. You must kiss all the children for me and tell them that I love them all and will come home when I kill all the Yankees. Dick Sanders says you must present his very best respects and compliments to all the girls of his acquaintance in old Rusk County and tell them that he hopes to see them soon again. This is from your devoted husband.

W. J. Whatley

1. WJW had moved to Clarendon, Arkansas, on the White River. *The Encyclopedia of Arkansas History & Culture* describes the White River as "an important byway for the Union forces and heavy with gunboat traffic and skirmishes, with Clarendon serving as a skirmish point. Confederate forces were decisively defeated there in July 1862 by Union forces under General Curtis whose march on Clarendon expanded Federal control of the area."

2. Stephanie P. Niemeyer and David Park, "McClarty, John," *Handbook of Texas Online*, accessed November 27, 2017. http://www.tshaonline.org/handbook/online/articles/fmcai; Stephanie P. Niemeyer, "Noble, Sebron Miles," *Handbook of Texas Online*, accessed November 27, 2017, https://tshaonline.org/handbook/online/articles/fno32.

"I had hoped that you would get along smoothly."

WJW urges her to accept her lot, not to expect much from Miller . . . Warnings to the "Negroes" . . . Punishment threats . . . Particular admonition for Marshall . . . Still waiting for clothing . . . WJW homily on religion and profane soldiers.

Camp Hope Arkansas
October the 12th 1862

My Dear wife,

I have this day received a letter from you dated the 22nd and 27th and mailed on the 1st of this month which is the 2nd letter that I have received from you since I left home. I was very glad to hear from you and to hear that you were all well, but am disturbed in mind to learn that you are frustrated and unhappy. I had hoped that you would get along smoothly. I fear from the way you write that Mr. Martin is not doing a good part by you. It seems that they have done mighty little since I left you. Mr. Martin promised me when I left that he would attend to my business and do the best he could, and I am very sorry to hear that [he] is becoming negligent, if such is the case, but I do hope my dear wife that you will pause and reflect and consider well your condition. You must not expect too much at his hands. You must be cool and considerate and not suffer your passions to rise above a level. Surely he will do right. But if you think he is not doing his duty or somewhere near it you had better quit and try it by yourself or go to your fathers or any other way that suits you and you think best, for I had rather sacrifice everything that we have than for you to be dissatisfied in mind. I have written to you before on the subject and advised you the best I was able, and I now say to you that you may use your own discretion in the matters and do what you think is best. Your pa can and will advise you for the best. I want you to tell the Negroes that if they don't go ahead with their work and do right and behave themselves while I am gone that I will certainly call them to an account when I come home, and I may be there before they look for me. I am having a harder time than any of them and if they won't behave themselves and work while I am gone that they need not expect any favors from me. Tell Marshal that I will hold him accountable for his bad conduct. I told him to stay at home and see to everything about the place and if he wants to call me master any longer that he had better do it. Our regiment just returned yesterday evening from White River near Clarendon [140–50 miles round trip] where we stayed three or four days, and were three days going and the same in returning and had a very hard time. I assure you we had three very hard rains on us and got everything we had wet, and slept wet for three nights. We were literally worn out with soreness and fatigue. We marched about eighteen miles in one day in Grand Prairie where we waded mud and water all day from the mouth to knee deep and it cold and raining the most of the time. Some of the boys give out with fatigue but they are getting in and no one much sick from it. For my part I am so sore today that I can scarcely get about. I wrote to you from our camp up there and thought at that time that we would remain there some time, as we were fortifying, but a private here is very short sighted and can't know but little, for we were soon ordered back to this point where we are tolerably well situated. I have plenty of good water and I reckon are getting as good as soldiers deserve. I do not have to know or pretend to know how long we will be here. We may winter here or we may leave here in three hours. We are having some cool weather now mighty nigh frost this morning and I think from the way air feels this evening that we will have it in the morning. The boys that went home on furlough are getting in now and will all be in soon that are able. I understand from them that our clothing will start for this place soon, and the boys some of them begin to need them. I don't think I will need anything more this winter except a shirt or two and I may possibly need a pair or two of socks, for socks don't last me now like they did when I was riding. I wore holes into a right new pair one days march through the mud and water. I wrote to you to send my coat if you had a chance. I would also like to have my India rubber [poncho, a precious item] if I could get it. I fear I will have to have some more bedding but that we can't carry when we travel and if we go into winter quarters I will try and make arrangements to get something here that will answer for you will have enough to do if you can clothe all you have with you. I hope you will be patient and bear our separation with fortitude and do the best you can be satisfied and not suffer things to trouble you that you cannot avoid. I would like to see you and be with you and hold you once more to my bosom with our little group around us, but as I am debared that pleasure for the present, let us live in hopes that the time will speedily arrive when God permitting we can be together to enjoy our own domestic happiness under our own vine and fig tree. I want you if you have any opportunity to see an artist to send me your likeness. I would be very glad to have it, to look at during my leisure moments. I am truly glad to hear that you have had some good meetings [revivals] in the neighborhood and also to learn that some of my relatives and friends are interested about their soul's salvation. I should like to have been there the best in the world, for here we are denied the privilege of listening to the word of god, but blessed be his name we can worship him as well in the army as anywhere and he has said in his promise that where two or three meet together in his name and agree as touching one thing it shall be granted. We have some good pious soldiers here but a great many profane ones. I am sorry to hear of the sickness in the neighbourhood and death of Miss Johnson. Thad got a letter from his mother today that stated that Billy Miller was dead also. I sincerely sympathize with Mr. And Mrs. Miller in their affliction. We have not drawed any more money yet. I have done all I can for Miller until the next draw. Don't fail to write to me soon. You must answer all my letters and tell all my friends to write to me. Give my love to the little children and tell them to be good children. My love to you all.

Adieu wife.
WJ Whatley

"I am still [in] the land of the living."

In camp . . . Settling complex personal debts . . . Camp Hope renamed Camp Nelson.

Camp Nelson Arkansas[1]
Oct 17th 1862

My Dear Wife,

I seat myself this evening to write you a few lines to let you know that I am still [in] the land of the living and in my usual health. I have nothing of any importance to write, and would not write, but have an opportunity of sending this by hand as Mr. Bromley will leave here in the morning for Texas. He lives near Henderson, our county treasurer. You will find in this letter twenty dollars for Mr. Miller which you will pay over to him and tell him it is all the money that I have of his or can get until we make another draw. Thirteen dollars and seventy five cents of it is from L.A. Treadwell which pays him out, five dollars from Lieut Weatherley which is the balance of eighty five dollars he collected, one dollar and twenty five cents from T.S. Coltharp which pays up all he owes. Tell him that I received his letter a few days since, and responded to it immediately answering all his enquiries to the best of my ability, and in that letter I sent him the Al Thomas note as I did not know at that time that I would have any chance to send it by hand. Lewis Elliott started home a few days since on sick furlough but Lt Gen. Holmes refused to sign it for him and he had to come back and I don't know whether he will get off or not. We are at our same camp but the name has been changed to Camp Nelson after the departed and much lamented General Nelson who died here about two weeks since. The remainder of Robert's regiment who were left behind have just got in today and looking in pretty good health.

1. Camp Hope was renamed in honor of Brigadier General Allison Nelson, "much lamented" according to William Whatley. Nelson was a prototype of mobility. Born in Fulton County, Georgia, he raised a unit for the Mexican War, the Kennesaw Rangers, served in the Georgia legislature, and became mayor of Atlanta. He moved to Kansas and became involved in the proslavery movement. From there he settled in Bosque County, Texas, near Waco, and was active in the secessionist movement in Texas. He raised a unit from the Waco area, the Tenth Cavalry. He served in Arkansas and died at Camp Hope of typhoid in late 1862.

OCTOBER 19, 1862
NFW TO WJW

"I will not grumble for I know that you
are engaged in a just cause."

A hint of patriotism from NFW . . . NFW lacerates Mr. Martin on several counts . . . He ignores her suggestions . . . She's had enough of him . . . An independent course . . . She shows she has mastered the farm operation . . . Six months later Martin still has not repaired her well . . . She won't move unless forced to.

Oct the 19th/ 62
At Home Rusk Cty Texas

To My Husband who is absent in reality but present in memory

I received your kind letter of the 20th inst. It come to hand yester-day. Also the one you wrote on the 13th. Just while on your way to your regiment I received also one that you sent by Mr. Morris about ten days ago. I paid Mr. Miller money over to him also the 100 to Pa as I had no use in the world for it. This leaves us all well except Marshal who is complaining some this evening but there is not much the matter with I do not think. The weather has been quite cool for two weeks sometimes cold enough for a fire all day. I assure you that when the cold begins to pinch me I think of the men that have left their homes to defend our rights & liberties & more than all the rest of my dear husband whose absence I feel so much but I will not grumble for I know that you are engaged in a just cause. I am so very lonely at night now that the nights are getting so long but I work the hardest to drive away my melancholy. You requested me to write to you about your affairs. I will proceed to do it to the best of my ability, in the first place the negroes have just hauled up the fodder & put up the fence on the creek. They gathered what seed peas there was & that was not many they did not mature. There has been nothing done since you left here but gather the crop. I have not got my crib full of corn it will take three more loads to fill it at least we made 92 loads of corn but they were not all good loads & the last of the corn was the lightest I ever saw except that dry year. There has been no rain of any consequence. Since you left we had two rains & if I could have gotten my turnips sowed the first rain they would probably have been better but part of the patch has never been sowed at all it was not fenced for three weeks. After it was sowed and the hogs rooted up at least half that corn up I suggested to Martin several times that it had better be fenced but he did not do it & accordingly I put the negroes at it myself as he would not do it. He has not been over to see to anything for two weeks & I do not know whether he intends to see to your business any longer or not. If he took offence at that I cannot help it for it was not only my privilege but my duty to see to my own affairs if he would not do it. There has not been anything done towards preparing the ground to sow grain. I put some of them to sprouting two or three days ago. He made the pass to have it done. I sent him word today that I wanted him to come over tomorrow morning & I shall find out what his notions are for if he is not going to take hold & manage I would like to know it. I have been trying to get him to fix my well for me but he has not done it yet. He said that he was going to find it the next week after you left but it was not done & he does not say he will or will not & I will never ask him again. He has his fixed now & does not care. I am going to go ahead to the best of my ability now & not wait for him if he is disposed to do what is right & will take hold all right but I have paid no attention to the whim he is in. I have followed your advice with regard to him in every particular & have been determined from the first that I would not give offence by anything there has never been anything done to the cross fence yet but if he does not see to it I intend to put them to fixing it in the morning. The fence by the old orchard field is the one that I speak of. I am very anxious that he will do right & attend to your farming if he will. You wanted to know how many turnips we had sowed there is probably 2 or 2½ acres sowed in the new ground & this patch at the house. I sowed it over again as there was not two days in that come up in it because it lay too long after the rain before it was sowed they are just not [growing] up now and will make greens but too late for turnips some say that there will be plenty of mast to fatten pork but I think that there is not. John Strange says there will be if there is not I do not know what I will do for I am satisfied that I will not have corn to fatten my pork & keep my hogs & pigs alive next summer. You say in your last that you do not fully understand my notions about moving but your notions & mine are the same for I have never intended to move as long as there was any sort of a show for me to stay at home but I never had intention of leaving there. They [stock] stay here I will stay with them, but I thought that in the event that I did have to go that I had rather have your notions about the matter & if I do have to go I want to move everything that can be moved stock & all except hogs they would not stay with me & that was the reason that I wanted to leave some one to attend to them if I was forced to go from home. I am as much averse to going away as you possibly can be. I have never intended to leave home until I was forced to do it. I shall still push on at home with the [farm] & try & [unreadable] for another crop & if I should have to leave I will make the best arrangement that I can.

"Our boys are doing tolerable well."

News about sick in camp... WJW learning to cook... Camp pranks... Wants news of crop yields... Detailed instructions... Bale and sell the cotton... Distributions to their creditors... Save cotton seed, keep it dry... More reports and rumors about another Corinth battle... Pessimistic... New Texas regiments arrive... All regiments understrength.

Camp Nelson Arkansas
October 21st 1862

My own true love

I have just received your letter of the 11th inst and I need not say that I was glad to hear from you for it is only the third that I have received from you since I left and have written you ten letters. [Note: NJW's letter dated October 11 did not survive.] You did not say how many you had received from me up to the time you wrote. I suppose this is in answer to the letter I wrote by Isaac Morris as you acknowledge the receipt of the money I sent by him. I am glad it got home safe. I wrote to you about four or five days since by Mr. Bromley and sent Mr. Miller twenty dollars in that letter which I directed him to mail at Henderson when he got home if he had no chance to send it by hand. I am still in good health, our boys are doing tolerable well, but we have some sick, Joseph Galloway, Lieut. Burnett and two or three others are at the hospital. Patrick is at the hospital cooking for the sick. R.G. Sanders and the rest of the boys of your acquaintance are all well and doing finely. We are now drawing beef and molasses, but our beef is not good. I am learning to be a pretty good cook, can make pretty good flour bread without lard, soda, or milk and think will be able to learn you something in the art of cooking by the time

I get home, but have not learned to love it yet, and fear I never will. There is a pigeon roost about seven miles from here about eight miles long and two miles wide where there are a great abundance of the birds and the boys slip out occasionally and go down and get a supply,[1] I have not been down yet and don't know when I will as we now have pretty tight guard duty to perform. Some of the boys cut off the tail of Col Lucet's horse which made him mad and caused him to put out an additional brigade guard of eighty men with instructions not to let any one pass without a pass from him or the Division commander, but some of them will go out notwithstanding. You did not write to me what you were doing nor how you were getting along with your matters. I would like to know [how] your corn turned out and peas and what kind of mast you had, whether you will have to fatten your hogs or not. You wrote me that the cotton had been sent to the gin. As soon as it is baled you have [Mr. Miller?] turned over to him and take up any indebtedness with him. He is to have three bales weighing five hundred each. The balance you must have brought home and taken care of, what you don't need to spin, and you had better have the seed hauled home if you have not done so and put up and kept dry, for seed, for if you don't use them next year you will need them sometime for the war will not last always. I hear news that there has been an engagement between Price, Van Dorn, and the federal forces near Corinth, the particulars of which I cannot give as we have had contradictory reports but the last one was that our forces were victorious which I hope is the case but am afraid not.[2] Col Speight's regiment [Fifteenth Texas Infantry] got in a few days since from Texas, and we are daily expecting Allens and Waterhouse's [Nineteenth Texas Cavalry, Dismounted] which was at Little Rock a day or two since. I find some friends and acquaintances in every Texas regiment here and we have now about twenty here, but they are not all full and some of them not more than half full.

22nd [October 1862] As I had to quit my letter yesterday evening to go out on dress parade I resume it this morning with another date and I shall have to be out this morning on review at 9 oclock and shall have to hasten this to a close. Our Texas troops here are under General [Henry] McCulloch who is acting Major general by Seniority, only Brigadier by appointment. I don't know how long we remain here, you will continue to direct your letters to Little Rock until I inform you otherwise. Write to me what Jessee is going to do and when he expects to go in the Service again. I'm glad to hear of Colleys good luck, and would be glad to see him in camp and good health. I was sorry to hear the sickness of little John [his son] but glad to hear that he is well and if you should take the measles you must remember to have them well nursed, and give as little medicine as possible, you know that your Pa's family went through them without much medicine or trouble. I do hope that the Lord will be merciful to you and permit you all to enjoy a reasonable share of health while I'm gone. I often think of you and my little children and pity your lonely condition, you must not let my little Mary forget her pa. I know the ballance will not. I shall now have to cut the letter off at half of what I intended to write, to go on Brigade guard as one of the guard detail is sick. So you see that a soldier is a creature of circumstance. I will write to you when I can and will want to hear from you regular, you must give me all of the news at home in detail. Farewell dear wife and children.

W. J. Whatley

1. WJW missed seeing the passenger pigeons, one of the marvels of American natural history. In 1862, several billion passenger pigeons flooded the flyways of the Mississippi Valley and lived in the forests. They darkened the skies wherever they went. By 1900, hunters had exterminated them. The last one died in 1914.

2. WJW was correct in his skeptical estimation of the rumor. After a successful early effort to recover Corinth, Van Dorn delayed his attack only to encounter prepared Union forces under William Rosecrans. Soon Van Dorn retreated, reprising his Pea Ridge leadership failure.

"Write often & lengthy for I get very anxious to hear from you."

Health news . . . Marshall has measles . . . Neighbor calamities . . . Sister Jane may have consumption . . . Argues for Mr. Miller . . . Rudely treated by Martin . . . Sending him clothes . . . Rampant hogs . . . Screwworms in the mules.

Oct the 26th/62
At Home Rusk Cty Texas

Dear Husband,

I seat myself this lovely Sunday evening to write you a few lines to let you know we are getting along which is bad enough in your absence but as well as could be expected now. I am glad that I can say to you that we are all well except for Marshal. He has measels has been sick some ten days. They are going in on him. He has had a very light attack [and] if the rest get off as well as I think he will I will be very thankful for I dread them but I will not physic them no way. It can be final for it is certain death is it is done. There is not A family but there is more or less sickness. It is measels. Mr. Mills wife is very bad off yet her general health is bad & she has had two very severe attacks of fever since you left home & it is almost out of the question to get quinine to break A case of fever none have any except Hubbard. I have just come from Mr. Russels. Al Thomas child is dead & died about noon today had measels & it fell on its lungs & as they had been affected by that spell of Scrofula it had last summer. It could not stand it. I have some bad news for you. Sister Jane has the consumption or at least her general health is on the decline & Pa thinks it is that he was down here last week to see Marshal & he said unless there was A change & that soon for the better he was satisfied she could not live long. She has got to be very feeble. We have been having some cold weather had as hard A freeze last night as we had all last winter. Have had no rain yet and there is no prospects of any now. Mr. Miller is going to take the hands & tend both farms just as Martin did. He has not acted the gentleman & I will never respect him such for no gentleman would talk to A lady as he did to me & I told him so. It was only about my hogs getting into his field. I had sent the negroes three times to fix the cross fence but they did not do it & I did not go to see about it myself for I sent Marshal the last time & he told me it was up good. Mr. Martin tore my hogs up with the dogs & beat them & after he done me all the harm he could in that way he came over & told that he would not stand it but would kill all of them if I did not keep them out of his pasture & marshall being picked took the boys & fixed it up immediately. I am sore from that two days work yet & I did it several days ago. He is the only man that I ever wanted you to thrash & I would have been glad if you could have happened in when he was going on so I think you could [have] cooled him down & if you ever get back I want you to treat him with contempt for I assure you he deserves it. His wife heard what he said & she hated it very much. Me and her are friendly as ever but I don't think I will speak to him next time I see him. & I don't care if I never do see him again. He will not do to depend on. I assure you Mr. Miller will take hold immediately. I will send you some clothes when Thad goes. They will be rolled up with this so there will be no chance to get them misplaced. Coll[e]y could not carry your coat. I will send you tobacco as I get the chance. There will be some mast but not enough to do the hogs much good. They are running every-where after it. I have mine fed some to keep them gentle. I will have a great many pigs before long which I will try to save. My mules have had the worst sore mouths you ever saw. The screwworms got in the big mules mouth but I had them got out in a hurry I assure you. Dr. March got 150 screwworms out of A mans nose last Saturday. It is A certain fact. I did not let Mrs. Russel have the corn because I did not have it to share but as she would not let me rest about until I paid her some money I paid six dollars to buy corn with & 15 she wants more. I have written closely to save paper but you can read it I guess. Write often & lengthy for I get very anxious to hear from you. Do write often.

> Your true & affectionate wife
> NF Whatley

> "[I] weigh a hundred and seventy four pounds,
> which is more than I ever weighed before."

No mail . . . Worried she's ill . . . Measles? . . . He has a cold . . . Rumors of skirmish near Helena . . . Whipped the Feds . . . Fortification of Camp Nelson . . . Waiting for battle . . . Building winter quarters.

> Camp Nelson, Ark
> October 31st 1862

My own dear wife

You must know the anxiety I feel about you when I say to you that the mail has been twice in since I have received a letter from you, bringing letters to a great many from your own [post] office but not a scratch for me. Oh why is this, is it the fault of the mail, or are you sick? I fear the latter for I know you would not fail to write for any other cause, and the last letter I received from you was written on the 11th inst and came to hand the 22nd stated that you expected you would all have measles soon and I have seen other letters from there that confirm what you stated. [Note: NJW's letter dated October 11 did not survive.] I responded to your last letter soon after its reception and gave you all the news I was in possession of. I am now suffering somewhat from a very severe cold which I have had for about ten days, and have had two chills, but they were light and I think they were from the effects of the cold. I am still up and about but feel a little weak. The sickness in our army is subsiding and have but few bad cases. We are now having some very fine nice weather fair and about cool enough to be pleasant. On last Saturday the 25th we had a very pretty little snow which preceded frost with us, the first I ever saw in October when the leaves were on the timbers. The next morning we had a pretty light freeze and fine spell for killing pork if we had had it. The orders have been officially read here from General Holmes requiring all men who were discharged under the Conscript Law to return and serve out their twelve months and ninety days. All men who belong to regiments on the other side of the river are required to report to head quarters and be ready to take up the line of march when ordered. We have also had the official report of an engagement lately between Capt Alph Johnson and the enemy down about hellena [Helena, Arkansas] killing about twenty & capturing seventy seven prisoners, thirty waggons, eighty mules & horses with the loss of only two wounded and one missing. (hurrah for Capt Alph) It is rumored here that there is or will be a call from Gen Lee for ten thousand Texas troops from this army but I do not give this as reliable. There are now sixteen Texas regiments here which are formed into four brigades. The cavalry have all left here and gone on white river and the Arkansas troops have gone up northeast but I do not know where they are located exactly. . . . [The rest of this letter did not survive.]

NOVEMBER 1862

"I am determined that I will not own a Negro of his age that will not take any interest in my affairs and let everything on the place go to rack."

Winter clothes and tobacco from NFW have arrived . . . WJW instructs on health care . . . Martin continues unreliable and eludes the draft . . . WJW urges NFW to get tough with the slaves . . . Money problems . . . News of Rusk County men in camp . . . Victory in Kentucky . . . Patriotic musings . . . Proud of NFW for weaving her own cloth . . . Admonishes children to do their chores . . . Bucolic farm-life dreams.

Camp Nelson Arkansas
November 2nd 1862

My Dear absent love,

Your welcome letter came to hand yesterday evening by John Colley, who arrived safe in camp and is looking finely, and were all very glad to see him, indeed it seemed almost like meeting with a member of ones family. I have just written to you two days ago, would not write to you now but to let you know that he had got in and I now acknowledge the receipt of two splendid shirts, some tobacco, and a fine candle for which I thank you heartily, and it shows to me that I am still remembered and am in the hearts of my little family. I have now got clothing, plenty to do me until next spring and I reckon shirts enough to do me twelve months unless I should happen to loose some of them. I have already written to you about my coats, which I shall need if I can get them (my rubber especially). I got a couple pair of socks that I left with the boys which will make me perfectly easy on that score. I was very glad to hear that you were still well and hope you will remain so. I got a letter from your pa by Colley also in which he stated that if you took the measles that he would stay with you and help you as much as he could and perhaps it may be best for you all to have them for you can never have them any younger and they will be as light on you now as at any future time. You must recollect that the least medicine is best in measles and there are more killed than cured by it. In regard to your matters at home, I am sorry to hear that you and Mr. Martin get along so badly and must confess that I am astonished to hear that he is acting towards you in the manner he is. I left him to see to my business and to take care of what little I had, instead of trying to tear up and destroy it. If the hogs got into his field, the Negroes were at his command to have them turned out and the fence put up. I presume they got in anyhow where he burnt up the fence. He ought to recollect that I fattened a gang of shoats for him last year and never hurt a hair on them nor had a hard word for I did not now blame a hog for going into a field for corn especially where there is no fence. I do not blame you at all for the way you have acted if he would not attend to business. You were necessarily compelled to take it out of his hands and see to it yourself, and I expect under existing circumstances you can do as well or better without him. But I do not want you to become excited and create any disturbances about it but merely tell him you have concluded to attend to your own affairs and I want you to ask Cousin Sladen for me to come down once and a while and see you and advise with you and keep the Negroes straight if they need it and I know he will do it for I know if I have a friend in that country he is the man. I think Mr. Miller will also give you any advice you need at any time in his power, and as I have told the Negroes how to do and admonished them time and again. If they don't go ahead and do right, you must have them corrected and made to do and Cousin Sladen will do that for you if you will ask him for it will never do for them to fool away their time and make nothing and if Marshall has got to wasting his time and running about and neglecting his business so you are not satisfied with him, you may hire him out if you choose, provided you can get anything for him and be sure you hire him to someone that will make him work, or if you could exchange him for some good stud negro (such as for instance as Cousin Syl's George) and pay some difference it would be a very good arrangement. I think you could get along very well, or if he won't do to suit you and you cannot make an arrangement such as either of the above, I am ready to sign a bill of sale to him at any time, provided he will bring anything like his value, for I am determined that I will not own a Negro of his age that will not take any interest in my affairs and let everything on the place go to rack when I am out undergoing twice the toil and fatigue and privations than any Negro I have seen at home. I am in earnest about what I write. I think we can live without him and am willing that he be sold at any time and payed on our debts, for if they don't work now it will not do to have them, for we can't feed and clothe them. We have not made a support this year and debts and tax both to pay. I will not be able to save much here for our wages has now been cut down to infantry, and according to the prices we have to pay here for everything a soldier needs it will about take his wages. We had not drawn any more since I came back here and I don't think now that we will soon for orders have been received to pay out no more money until all the troops are paid up to the 31st of June, the time we were paid up to. I have, however, about eighty dollars which will be a plenty to answer my purpose until another draw until I should happen to get sick and if I do I will have difficulty getting more. I have not had any more chills since I wrote to you last but am still feeling somewhat weak from them which is not broke up with me yet entirely. I think I will be stout again soon. I have just returned from a visit with Colley and to see James Walker and some of the other boys in other regiments. Jimmy got his letters and seemed very glad to hear from home as it was the first letter he had had since he left home. He is in tolerable good health. I am doing very well. L.B. Elliott is out of the hospital and John waiting on him. I don't think he is very bad off, but I have not seen him myself. Our boys are looking about as well as I ever saw them since we have been fairly inducted into the service. We now have ten companies in our regiment. We got Capt McKnight's company from Ochiltree's regiment as he had eleven companies. He is brother to Wm McKnight who married Susan Wynne. And if we should now get all who were discharged from our company & regiment at the reorganization we will have a very good regiment. But it is now very small no more than seven or eight hundred in all and not much more than five hundred who stay in camp and do duty. The last no. of the Confederate News gives us a complete victory in Kentucky, if true, and it could in so many ways that I am inclined to believe it.[1] The waggons are now being repaired at the yard and mules shod preparatory to moving at a moments warning which some think will be before many days, but it is only a surmise with them, however if we do not spend the winter here we will certainly not remain here much longer, and General Holmes says that we need not think of winter quarters for they are not admitted in his vocabulary. For my part I am reconciled to undergo almost anything in the bounds of reason for a short time if not taxed beyond my strength to gain our rights and liberties and once more be permitted to return home as free men to the bosoms of those we love, for I do think if we are successful and gain our independence that we will certainly know how to appreciate it. And while I am here battling in the cause it is certainly encouraging to me to hear that my own dear one at home is there nothing daunted plying the shuttle wheel & needle to maintain independence at home in domestic affairs [embargo on Northern clothing goods].[2] John, my son, you must be a good boy and learn to ride Freedom so you can go out and drive up the cows & sheep for your ma, but you must mind that you do not go too far at first and get lost. You must take care of the little lambs and not let them suffer and die for we will want a heap of wool for clothes. You must make Marshall take the wagon and go with him to cousin Sladens after the one he gave your ma if she has not sent for it. Arch must go and make them feed the hogs and make the little negroes attend to the calves and he must learn to ride too so he can go over to Mr. Miller's for anything you want him to carry or bring. Jane must feed the chickens and raise a heap so that when I kill all the Yankees and come home she can have me a plenty of eggs & chickens to eat. And little Mary must run for wood and be as sweet as she can so as I can get a sweet kiss from her when I come home. I don't hear any talk now about furloughs this winter, but if we don't move soon I think it is likely that some of the boys will get to come home. It is reported that Hindman has been fighting above here and has sent for Gen. Holmes to reinforce him and it is thought that if we go up that way we will go to Fort Smith. Our army is moving on now with some system & discipline. The drum beats in the morning at six to get up, again at 9 to drill and we drill company drill from that time till eleven. We are then dismissed until two when the drum beats again for Battalion drill until half after 4 and beats again at five or sunset for dress parade where all the orders we have are read to us by the adjutant of the regiment. The drum again beats at eight o'clock P.M. for all to be in camps and asleep by nine after which there is to be no loud talking or hallowing. There was a sermon preached this evening at headquarters but not being advised of it until he had commenced, and I had been engaged in writing to you I did not go out to hear him. Colley gives a glowing account of the many fine meetings you have had in your midst of which I was very proud to hear and would like to have been with you. I would to God that we could have some such in this western army for if there ever was a people that needed religion certainly we do. I sometimes al-most fear that the lord will overthrow us in our wickedness. Colley tells me that he don't think you have ever got either of the papers I sent you. I wish you would inform me that I may write to the Editor about them and see into the cause. Write to me as often as you get my letters and you know what I want hear about. You must not use your paper in waste for I am afraid it will be hard to get any more. If I should need any more I will let you know. To now be debared the pleasure of writing to you and hearing from those I love would be next to death. The order has just been read on dress parade that Col Culberson of Ochiltree's reg has been ordered to bring up the men who will discharged under the conscript act to come to their companies serve out their term of enlistment.

Write soon and often to your beloved
W. J. Whatley

1. In August 1862, Braxton Bragg took the war to Kentucky to relieve pressures on Vicksburg and Middle Tennessee. The CSA was successful in every encounter with Union forces and Kentucky went for the Confederacy, but Bragg, after Van Dorn's defeat at Corinth, took his army back to Knoxville. The campaign was a strategic failure for the Confederacy.

2. WJW rhapsodizes NFW spinning and weaving. The embargo on Northern cloth and the admonition to Southern women to spin their way to independence soon exhausted the supply of cards, which the South could not replace.

7 NOVEMBER 1862
NFW TO WJW (FRAGMENT AND DAMAGED)

"There is more children dying now than I ever hear of before in my life."

Measles epidemic among children and slaves . . . Diphtheria! . . Drought continues . . . Arson in main pasture . . . Troubles with livestock and slaves.

At Home Rusk Cty Texas
Nov the 7th 1862

My Dear Husband

I seat myself to drop you a few lines as I have an opportunity of sending it by hand as Mr. Davis is going to your camp with a wagon carrying clothes to the soldiers. This leaves the family well with the exception of measles. Lillie, Harriet, and Susan all have them now or broke out now. Marshal is about well. I think they did not hurt him much. None of the rest [slaves] have them yet but I hope not. I doubt but what they will be sure to have them. There is more children dying now than I ever hear of before in my life. Janie lost her babe last Sunday. Some say that it was fever, some say measles. I did not know that it was sick until it was buried, was sick only about four days. Cousin Syl lost a little negro last week with croup. This bad sore throat is prevailing through the country now and is fatal in three fourths of the cases. We are now having some cool weather. It is clear and dry. I never saw the ground as dry in life, not even that dry year. There is no appearance of rain at all. Some are sowing grain where the land is loose enough to plow but you can hardly see them for the dust that rises around the plow. For my part there cannot be a plow stuck in the ground until it does rain. My hogs are falling off from what they have been. I thought that I would put the large ones up and feed them for it will be a losing business to let them get thin and then fatten again. I shall kill them as soon as they get fat enough and the weather permits. I killed that black steer yesterday and I never saw such a beef in my life unless it was from the prairie. And it was fatter than one half of them. I do wish that you had some of him for I know that it is better than that you have in camps. Someone one set the march field on fire and burnt up a great many rails and the fire spread and burnt out the range so the cattle will be the worse for it. They are poorer than I ever saw them in my life I think. I will be sure to loose some of mine but will spare no pains to keep them alive for I have already had so much trouble with some of them that the screwworms were at work on that. I will be more loath to loose both labor and stock for I assure you that you have nor can you have no idea what trouble they have caused me unless you could have seen for yourself. I know that in. . . . [letter breaks off, page missing, tears]

"There will be insurrectionary movements about Christmas . . .
there are three negro men to one white one now. . . .
the women will be left to their mercys."

*Jane has measles and wants her "pa" to nurse her . . . Drought continues . . .
NFW's melancholy about her children's bleak future . . . Local deaths, mostly
children . . . Mr. Miller's fiscal and legal troubles . . . Marshall confronts Mr.
Miller with "saucy jaw" . . . Fair potato crop . . . Cards wearing out from ac-
celerated home weaving . . . Rumors of Jayhawker raiders in nearby Smith
County . . . NFW in terror about the "negroes" . . . Begs WJW to get a furlough
and come home.*

Nov the 9th 1862 Caledonia Rusk cty Texas

My Dear Husband

I seat myself to drop a few lines to let you know how we are getting
along. Jane is not well is taking the measles, I think. She has had
fever ever since yesterday morning. It is not altogether as high as
it has been, I think, will be broke out in the morning. George has
also taken it since I wrote to you last. I think that I will be able to
manage them very easily unless they assume a more malignant form
than they have as yet. I have not had any symptoms of them yet
and hope that I may escape until the rest get pretty much through
so that I may indeed. It is so very dry that it is impossible to plow
in my field & it would run a greater risk than I am willing to run to
sow wheat now. The ground as dry as it is. If it should happen to
come up, it would be sure to die unless it rained immediately, but
there is some little prospects of rain tonight & surely it will raise
soon. Some are sowing & risking it. John has just gone to bed. He
thinks as much of you as ever & often speaks of his absent Pa &

says he wants to see you mighty bad. Archie is at his Grandpa's. He went home with Isham [George Isham Watkins (1849–1930), one of NFW's younger brothers] this morning, will be at home in a day or two as Jane is coming down to stay with me some while. They are all sick & I often think of your kind attentions when any of them are sick. Jane is in bed asleep but is somewhat restless. She wants you to nurse her. She frequently tells me her pa is coming home to nurse her. Sister Mary grows very fast. She gets a string & puts it on a chair & tries to make a noise like a wheel. Poor children, they are seeing their happiest times now. They do not know the sad realities they will have to encounter in after life which will be sure to come sooner or later. There has been more deaths in the last four weeks than I ever heard of before in the same length of time in my life. I believe mostly children. Mrs. McGuire is dead. She died last week. I saw George McCoy four or five weeks ago. He looked about the same old George. He inquired after you & said he wanted to see you very bad. The weather is still cold. I do not think that I ever saw the first cold spell last as long in my life without some warm days & there has not been a single really warm day since it turned. Old Mrs. Miller is improving slowly so he told me today. Mrs. Miller is able to be up some of the time. I am afraid that Mrs. Russel & Pete Thomas will give Mr. Miller trouble about that money. They say that they are going to prosecute him for it & that there is two men in this neighborhood that will stand at her back & see her out in it but she will not give any names & he is very mad about Mr Russell writing there that he said that the boys had acted rascally with him. He denies it & she says that he said it & she will swear it any day. Mr. Miller was talking about Al trying to cheat him out of what was justly his & demeaning him for it & said that the boys, some of them, had acted rascally with him & she asked him if Thad had acted dishonest too. He told her there was eighty dollars paid by someone. He did not know who had paid it. If Thad it was all right. If not he was with the rest of them that they might have all sent money by Mr. Murphy. He is very mad about her writing that back there. She did it to injure him as they say openly & aboveboard that they intend to do him all the harm they can both here & there. Some thinks that they can make him smoke for it. I do not know. What I write to you is Mr. Miller's tale to me this evening. Delie Thomas was here when he brought the letter you wrote to him over for me to read & said in her presence that there was a lie written back there & she did not say anything to him for when I saw him coming she said she was going to give him a good one & I told her not to say anything to him out of the way as it was in my house. She must go to his house to do that & she did not say anything all but says she is going to see him this week. But enough of others business. I am fearful Mr. Miller will have trouble with Marshal as he gave him some saucy jaw this evening about what he told him he had to do in the morning & Mr. M. threatened to take his shirt & he waited until he got out of his hearing & said he would never be whipped by him. He did not intend to be controlled by him neither no farther than he wanted to. He has been trying to get me in a good humor all the week & does not want you to hear of his misdemeanors. The fact he has done as he pleases so long he thinks he is not to be controlled at all but if Mr. Miller will only be firm with him he will soon find out who he has to deal with. He says upon the first provocation he will show him white is white. I want you to write to me very often & write long letters for there is nothing on earth that affords me half as much pleasure as to hear from my dear darling husband. If you can only be spared to come home I will try to bear our separation by mail. John wants to know what you do about a gun if you have one, what sort it is.[1] He seems very much interested about whether you have anything to fight with or not. I heard from Pa's yesterday. John and [?] went up there. They were up & about. Pa & Jesse had gone to Kaufman to buy Uncle John's place that he left so Ann told John that was the first that I had heard of it consequently do not know what their notions are for it. We made some thirty or forty bushels of potatoes. I have half of them for seed as I wanted seed enough one time and try next year with a fair chance & see what I can do. I am trying to make as much cloth as I can. My cards are giving out & where the next is to come from I do not know. It is reported here now that the Jayhawks are coming in on the people in the western & northern counties & killing as they come to them & plundering them of what they want.[2]

It is said that they have come as far in as Smith County [sixty miles from Caledonia] & were caught & hung but we do not know what to believe about it. Some think that there will be insurrectionary movements about Christmas but as yet I see no indication of that yet but I do hope that it will prove a false alarm for if that be the case we are in a helpless condition indeed for there are three negro men to one white one now & the others are already enrolled & that will reduce the number to such an extent that they will be nothing in their way & the women will be left to their mercys. I want you to be sure & write to me often for I am a great deal better satisfied when I can hear from you regularly & things do not trouble me near as much as then as when I cannot get letters from you & I get in a melancholy way & look at the dark side of everything. Do not think that I am complaining of you for such is not the case but want you to continue to write often. I have gotten your letters up to the 11th of last month & have responded to them. The ones written on the [unreadable] & 11th come together & the one from Clarendon come last. It came to hand about four days ago. I want you to try & get a furlough & come for Christmas if you can so you can see how things are going on here. Tell Dick I did as he requested me & they send their best respects and wishes for his welfare. Tell Colby that his negroes have the measles but are getting along very well. Bill was the only one that I know that had them not that mean are the other Bill [last five lines destroyed]

 N. F. Whatley

1. On children learning about weapons during the Civil War, see chapter 5 of Marten, *The Children's Civil War.*

2. For NFW, Jayhawkers inspired nightmares of marauding bands from Unionist Kansas and Missouri. Sherry Kidd, archives manager of the Smith County Historical Society, conducted a thorough search and did not find any such raids in Smith County during 1862. Kidd quotes from a Smith County chronicle as symptomatic of local attitudes in 1862—"the fear that Kansas 'Jayhawkers' might sweep through Indian Territory, cross the Red River, and commit murder and mayhem among the unguarded towns and plantations of eastern Texas." In 1864, the *Galveston News* reported a Jayhawker raid on Van Zandt County.

"This wicked and unnatural war . . .
I sometimes think this war will ruin us."

WJW in good health . . . Pain of separation . . . His Uncle George killed in Maryland . . . Laments the loss of so many good men . . . Blankets, winter clothing scarcity . . . Lots of marching—no shooting . . . NFW has fired Martin . . . Urges her to rely on Dr. Watkins . . . First mention of selling out and moving to town . . . Worried the war will impoverish them . . . Weary of camp life . . . And drums.

Camp Nelson Ark
November 9th 1862

Dearest Nannie

Your letter of the 26th just came to hand last night, and was welcomed to my heart as a dear treasure. I was very glad to hear you were in tolerable health, and as you have the measles now started I hope they will be light if they should continue with you. Was sorry to hear of Janes bad health, for I assure you she is a great favorite of mine. I am now in my usual good health. Just came off of guard this morning and I don't think I can employ a little leisure this morning any better than in writing to her I love. To hold sweet communion as it were by letter, Oh that I could see you and the little pets I love a little while this morning. I do know we could pass the time pleasantly. I never knew what it was to be separated from you before the inauguration of this wicked and unnatural war. God grant that it may be brought speedily to a close and permit us all to return once more to our loved ones at home. I saw a letter a few days since from Cedartown, Georgia which stated that Uncle George Whatley was killed in Maryland and one of my cousins got his leg shot off and a great many more of my friends were killed and wounded.[1] I would not be astonished to hear that some of my brothers have shared the same fate.[2] We have already lost a great many valuable lives and I fear we will have to make a still greater sacrifice before it is brought to a close. We have some news recently that is somewhat encouraging if true, but I do not rely on much I hear now for there is too many false rumors afloat, we are now ready to move at a moments warning, but do not know when that morning will come. I think it probable that we will winter somewhere in this section of country. The clothing for some of the regiment have come in and others expected soon. We have no correct information from ours yet but suppose it must be on the way before now. The boys will be glad to [have] them for some of them begin to need them. There is a great lack of blankets in camp. A good many have but one and it is impossible to keep comfortable in that condition. We are now having some of the prettiest weather I ever saw. Cool misty mornings and fair, pretty days. We have not had any rain on us since we got back from our trip to Clarendon, which was a hard one I assure you. I had rather fight two days any time than to march one such as we had while on that trip. Cousin Wm. Barney is up here in our brigade. He belongs to Sweets regiment [Fifteenth Texas Cavalry (Dismounted)], came here about the time I went home last summer. He is now out at a private house sick. He lay about four weeks in the hospital and has been out where he now is about four. He heard that I was here and sent for me to go to see him. I was out to see him twice last week. He was very glad to see me and seemed to do him a great deal of good, has been very low but is now improving slowly and I think that if he don't get a bad set back he will get well, but he has a keen apetite, and has just received a box of sweetmeats from home and there is danger of his eating too much. I advised him not to open it until he got better, and he promised me he wouldn't. I shall write to his father today, at his request and let him know how he is getting along, as he is not able to set up long enough to write himself. His younger brother (Thomas) he tells me is in Virginia in Terry's regiment [8th Texas Cavalry/Terry's Rangers] and in good health when he was last heard from. He says his father is doing well in Limestone and is very anxious that we should move out there when this war closes.[3] Tell Cousin Syl when you see him that Seaborn Gray is dead and Aunt [unreadable] is married again. She married a man by the name of Sweet. William says she is all lively as ever. Jimmy Walker is in good health. I saw him a few days since. Those regiments that have recently come up here have a good deal of sickness among them and a right smart of fatality. Captain C. P. Whitstone died about a week ago with pneumonia. He had a very severe attack, was only sick about four or five days. The health of our regiment is a great deal better than it has been. I think we will stand it now, if we have half a chance. I am writing to you this morning on a piece of an old letter. I have other paper but as I thought this would answer I would use it for I don't know how long I will have to write to you and next to seeing you it is the greatest pleasure I have. You write me that you and Martin have quit. I reckon you had done right for you were getting along very bad and your interest suffering greatly. I am sorry he acted so and betrayed the confidence I placed in him for when I left home I believed he would attend to my affairs. But I reckon the old adage is true and perhaps best which let each one on himself for assistance depend and shun all occasions to call on a friend, for you don't know how soon you may have it to do. You say you have got Mr. Miller to manage for you. I know he will do right but the men who enlisted last Spring now discharged have all been ordered back to the service to serve out their terms of enlistment which will bring him into the service again and break up that arrangement [the Conscription Act of September 1862 extended the maximum age to 45]. I understand however that the late law makes provisions for exempting any man who has 20 negroes where there is no white male on the place and he and I together has about that number and probably one or the other can be detailed to stay at home. You must do the best you can. Your Pa will know how to advise you for the best and will do it if you should fail in any arrangement to get some one with you, and you could sell our place or let old man Jones have it back if he should want it. I would be glad. We have a good place I know, but I am now in the service for the war, and you are some distance from any one who would take any interest in your affairs if Mr. Miller should leave, and consequently you would not get along well and be satisfied and you know if you should leave home that the place would go down very much. These are my reasons for wanting to sell out. You could then go and live near your pa and he could take care of you, and we could settle ourselves again after the war. I received a letter from your Pa by Colley and will answer it in this as you will see him soon and he can read it. I want you to consult him about your businesses and you and him just what you think is best and it will all be satisfactory with me. If you could be well situated and satisfied, it would please me very much. I sometimes think this war will ruin us, for we are owing money and are not making enough to pay the interest and I have concluded that it would be best to sell land if anything. But we will not let these things trouble us unnecessarily for it all goes in ones lifetime anyway. I fear you will not make any wheat again next year as it still keeps so dry that it will not do any good. I am sorry to hear that the mast is no better with you as you are scarce of corn. You had better not fatten too many hogs as some of them will be small and will take a great deal of corn to make pork out of them. I hope you have made potatoes as I hear that they [are] fine in some parts of the county. I am told that flour is very scarce and high in Texas so I reckon you are living hard enough. We are getting plenty here and are most all getting fat. Hogs are very scarce in this country and I fear we will not get much pork and turnips this fall and winter. Two more of our boys got in yesterday who were furloughed last summer. They have both been sick. Our officers are coming down on us pretty tight right now and some of the boys gamble a good deal but we have to stand square to the music, and I never was as tired of any thing in my life as I am of music, drums more especially for they are a signal here for almost everything that is done. Write to me if you get a Little Rock paper. I shall expect you to answer all my letters and hope you will do it promptly for I feel mightily down when the mail comes in and the other boys gets letters and I don't, but it has not been that way often. I have every reason to believe that my wife thinks as much of me as any of them. Tell the children I often think of them and would like very much to see them. My love to all relations and friends. I would like to have letters from some of them.

This from your devoted husband
W. J. Whatley

1. Captain George Croghan Whatley of Calhoun County, Alabama, died at the Battle of Antietam, September 7, 1862.
2. WJW's older brother, John Wilson Whatley, served in the Sixtieth Alabama Infantry, and Seaborn Jane Whatley, the youngest, was in the Tenth Alabama Infantry.
3. Limestone County, largely a blackland prairie area, is located near Waco and the Brazos River.

NOVEMBER 18, 1862
WJW TO NFW

"God grant that this war may soon close for there has already been enough widows and orphans left upon the homes of the world . . . carried much farther we will be a ruined people both North and South. . . . I don't want the negroes to eat any idle bread."

Camp life . . . He gets a lot of beef . . . Homesick . . . Health concerns and news . . . Peril of illness under CSA's primitive medical care . . . Peace rumors: France and England forcing an armistice . . . War has gone on long enough . . . Cotton cards in Searcy at inflated prices . . . Clothing shortage . . . Rain and leaky tents . . . Wants NFW by his side . . . Tender passage . . . "Be content" . . . Still battling for Southern rights . . . No tobacco . . . More domestic instructions.

Camp Nelson Arkansas
November 18th 1862

My darling Wife,

Again the mail has come in and I have received no letter from you but it will not deter me from writing to you for I know that you will want to hear from me, and as long as I can procure paper and other material, I will write to you. Over a week, or ten days shall not pass at any time without writing if I am able and have an opportunity. I am in pretty good health at present but have had a few spells and have been suffering since somewhat from cold. My mess are all up and able to eat their full rations which consist of bread and beef, but we are getting a plenty of that, and will be mighty thankful if it gets no worse. I believe that I love beef better than I ever did in my life before, and it is not the best I ever eat I assure you. I often think of you and the children at home and sometimes think that if I had something to eat prepared by your dear hands, it would do me a great deal of good. And I know it would if I could be with you and sup with you around our own board. I never knew before how well I loved my little family until we were separated and if it is the Lord's will that we may all meet again in this world, I think we will be properly prepared to enjoy a perfect felicity and if we should not be permitted to see each other again in this world, let us live so as to meet in our father's kingdom where we can join in singing his praise and be happy through eternity. The health of our army is not so good now as it has been there is a brain fever prevailing here which is killing a good many. We lost a man out of our company last Thursday (John C. Gillespie) from Bellview [now Pirtle, Rusk County]. James Wright of Brewton's company died last night, was only sick three days. Gustavus Treadwell was in Waterhouse's regiment yesterday and brought word that John Ray is dead. He died last Friday, only sick about twenty four hours. Gus is going back today to see his brother who is sick but he thinks he is not dangerous. A good many more have died but as you are not acquainted with any of them it is useless to enumerate them. Our regiment is not suffering as much as those other regiments that have lately come up. They are now moving all the sick to Little Rock who are able to go and building hospitals here for the balance. It is mighty hard for a man to get up here from a hard spell of sickness, from the fact they seldom get such attention as they ought to have. God grant that this war may soon close for there has already been enough widows and orphans left upon the homes of the world. There has been a good deal said lately about peace. It is rumored that England and France have acknowledged our independence and that the two governments are about entering an armistice for four months, and it is thought that will be sure to bring about peace, but these are only rumors.[1] It is true that a good deal of these reports are in the papers but that don't make it true. We want to believe it but are afraid. Such a thing is not at all impossible, for I think now is a very pretty time for peace if it comes any time soon, for they have certainly prosecuted this war far enough to know that they can never accomplish their object in subjugating the South, and if it is carried much farther we will be a ruined people both North and South. I have just heard that there are some cotton cards at Searcy about twenty five miles above here, and we are going to start a man up there today to see about it and buy several pair if they are there. I have sent for a pair for you and two if I can get them at ten dollars. It is said that they are only worth eight dollars, but I think it doubtful about their being there at all and if they are there I expect they will be worth fifteen or twenty dollars a pair. I do not know whether you have got any or not and if you have not I know you need them. And if I can get them I will have an opportunity of sending them to you by some of the wagons that came up to bring clothing to the regiments. The clothing is now coming in pretty fast. All the clothing for our regiment has come except for our company which will be in soon by a private wagon. None of our neighbor boys in Brewton's company have received any yet, but I think they are expecting them in the wagon that is coming to bring clothing for Capt Jordan's company in Roberts' regiment. It is raining a slow rain now and has been all day and in fact it has been raining more or less every day and night since Sunday morning. Our tents are too small for the men we have in them and are getting old and inferior which causes them to leak and situates us very disagreeable in such weather. I think when this warm, wet spell breaks up we will be apt to have some winter and then I know I shall think more about home than ever, for I have got no one here to lie close up to me and encircle me in the arms of love and protect me

from the cold. Yes, I will often think of thee and of thy oft told request to hug and kiss you and will surely regret that I am now denied
that happy privilege. But such is fate. It has become necessary for
me to be here to battle for the rights of my country and for the present we must be content and cheer up and look forward with much
pleasure to the time when I will return home once more and nestle
in the bosom of her I love better than all others besides, for I am and
will remain as true to thee here as thou art to me, and I know that
never was there a woman truer or more devoted to a husband than
my blood is to me. I dreamed a few nights since that you were with
me and I thought I was the happiest mortal on earth, but when I
woke and found my mistake my hopes were all blasted. We are still
at Camp Nelson and so far as I know will be here for some time. We
have had orders to be in readiness to move from here some time ago
but we may winter here, and may move tomorrow or even sooner.
The most of our time is occupied now, for there are so many roll
callings and so much drilling to do that we hardly have time to write
on any day except Sunday which is the only rest day we have, and
that not entirely for we have to go out in the morning to inspection
of arms and in the evening to be on parade so you can see that they
keep us stirring around nearly all the time. But if I can keep my
health I don't ask for any differences for I have got use to it. We are
very scarce of cooking utensils and have to have larger messes which
don't suit me. We have had ten men in our mess since I came back
which is twice as many as I want. They are all good fellows but it
takes too much cooking, and I don't love to do that. Washing is about
the hardest task. I have washed one shirt since I have been here and
rubbed the skin off my fingers and since that I have been paying a
bit a garment and think I am doing finely for some charge as high as
twenty cents. This country is getting tolerable scarce of every thing
that a soldier needs. We are nearly all out of tobacco now and have
to pay very high for all we get. The citizens bring in a little here occasionally and sell it from one to two dollars a plug which with a
little other spending money will about take all a soldiers' wages. I
learn that the freeze you had in Texas has pretty much ruined all the

acorns, and I fear that if you have to fatten your pork that you will be scarce of corn but I hope you will have enough to make out with. You have made a very good arrangement in getting Mr. Miller to attend to business for you (if he don't have to return again into the service) you can tell him about what improvements I want made about the farm, in the way of fencing and he will have it done. I want all my fence put in good repair before pitching another crop, and they must make an early and try and make a good crop. Cousin Syl Walker promised me two diamond plows [manufactured in Canton, Illinois] which you can send and get and I reckon by having the others worked on they can manage to make out and make a crop. I want them to try and cultivate that corner of bottom down next to the bridge next year. It is a mighty good piece of land and will make good stuff. I had hopes would have had the new ground fenced before now and if Mr. Miller thinks that they can manage it, I want it put in, for it will make a good crop of corn with but little work. I don't want the negroes to eat any idle bread next year for we need a good crop mighty bad. The stock must not be neglected. You had best keep them up this winter until lambing time is over and tell John he must feed them and give them all the bran from the kitchen and some salt. You must let him learn how to ride and he can go on errands for you and by sending someone with him a time or two he would soon learn the way to Mt. Enterprise and could go after and carry the mail for you which will save the time of someone else that will probably be worth something in the field and you must make your arrangements to put out all the help you possibly can in the spring while the crop is making for I want all my land cultivated that you have not seeded and I reckon that is but little if any for I understand it has been so dry that you can't sow grain. I want you to take good care of my shot gun and don't let it rust. You must have it rubbed up every damp spell of weather and keep it oiled. I left it loaded. You can have it shot off if you rather. You must be careful about accidents. I have just dined on head bacon and molasses, so you can see that we have drawed a little bacon in camp. We have been getting a little sugar and molasses heretofore and know if we had some flour we could have fine eating for a while. The boys always say when we begin to draw bacon that we may look out for more soon and begin to make ready right here. I have just been interrupted in my letter by a large gathering of men in one of the companies to our left to see two men fight but they have made it up now and nobody hurt but a little scratch on one countenance. The boys fall out and pop a few licks occasionally but they are sure to put them under guard for it and they don't have much fun at last. Company F has been entirely peaceable yet and I hope they will remain so. We have about the best cap [company commander] in the regiment. He is as kind to his men as he can be and understands the drill first rate. I have adopted this method of writing close in order to give you long letters on a little piece of paper. I have written to you so often from the same place that I have no news to write that you don't already know except to let you know from time to time the condition of my health and how I am getting along. I wish to hear in return all about how you are getting along with your affairs. I will write to you again when I get a letter from you. I hope you are well and will all keep on reading my letters to the children and tell them who it is from and where I am and don't let them forget me. Give my love to your pa and family. I am under many obligations to him for assurances that you will not want for anything. I would be glad to have a letter from him. I don't write to any one but you as paper is scarce and time short. Write to me soon and often and remember that this is from your love.

W. J. Whatley

1. Rumors were rife in the summer of 1862 that Great Britain and France would call for a truce or outright recognition of the Confederacy. The steady pressure of Ambassador Charles Francis Adams, the caution of Lord Palmerston, the popularity of Lincoln with the British proletariat, and the draw at Antietam with Lee's retreat into Virginia finished the subject of European intervention. WJW was accurate in his doubts.

"I see there is some prospects of peace & do hope that it is true."

Conscription law confusion . . . NFW wants to combine two families to get the twenty slaves required for an exemption to get WJW home . . . Sending WJW clothing . . . More on Martin . . . Worming the hogs . . . Peace prospects.

Caledonia, Rusk Cty Texas
Nov. the 21st 1862

Dearest heart of my heart,

I seat myself to respond to your letter of the 31st of Oct which I received today. It found us all up & I hope that this may find your health restored for I know it is bad enough to be sick at home & surrounded by home friends but is much worse situated as you are being deprived of many of the comforts of life & I know that no person would wait on you as I would. Jane is getting well, can sit up about half of the day & is able to walk about some. Little Arch is out of danger with care. In your last letter you said you did not receive letters as often as you ought. It is not my fault for I have written to you regular. I do not think that I missed two weeks at any time & have written weekly the most of the time & will continue to do so & if you do not receive them it will be in the fault of the mail. You may rest assured that you are on my mind both day & night. I frequently dream that you are with us & when I wake & find it is not a reality I am almost ready to wish that could dream on until you do come home. In your last letter you spoke of the nonconscript men having to go back that get into my arrangements again for it will take Mr. Miller. He thinks that it is not right for them to be recalled. After being sent home they come home and remained during the leisure season & when they could be of some benefit to their familys they have to leave. I do not know what to do next but will see Pa & hear what he says. So I think that according to the exemption bill you could be paroled to come home if you could get to attend to Mr. Miller's business. He has six negroes & we have thirteen & will soon have another that is all [on] the way that we can get one & you have as much right to come home as any one else. Write me immediately what you think about it. I think that I will get Pa to work the negroes together until some other arrangements is made. George Birdwell is with him yet & is going to stay until he is forced off [conscripted]. If we can make no better arrangement I will try it myself but I have not the judgment to carry it on to an advantage. If Mr. Martin would only acted right he would have benefited by it as well as me but if he was to undertake it again which he cannot as he will have to go too I would have no confidence in him for I know he fooled me this time. You want your coats sent you the first opportunity which I will do & some socks & tobacco that [we] will have to box. Mr. Martin promised me some for you & I went after it & he said that he would put you up four or five lbs. & I then sent to get some to send by Lolly that was all he could share. He said that was before he acted so badly but you shall have it. Cousin Syl got a letter from Jack. He is at Holly Springs, Miss & was well. Jimmy writes to his folks that he is in bad health & keeps them uneasy all the time. I am going to have my hogs worked on soon as the worms is so bad that I would have lost them to have it done sooner. The Jones hogs have done badly & have three pigs but the rest are dead I guess. I got one shoat but it was nearly dead as can be. I will have her put up soon. I wrote you how every thing had turned out in the crop line. I get the Little Rock paper regular also the Confederate News which is printed by Gould at Austin in the Austin paper. I see there is some prospects of peace & do hope that it is true. Ben Birdwell has come home. He is wounded in the foot & it is thought that he is a cripple for life. I am not informed as to what condition he left the other boys or where they are. I am in a hurry to get this to the office & will have to cut it short. You must write to me immediately.

From your loving wife
N. F. Whatley

"If you ever come back we can find another home somewhere else."

NFW in crisis . . . Rain at last and sowing grain! . . . Their lien holder wants the place back . . . Desperate about what to do . . . Burdensome debt and another year of war would be ruinous . . . What to do with the slaves? . . . Agonizing over the slaves she wants to retain . . . Slaves won't work . . . Men over forty being called up . . . Slaves arriving from the war zone . . . Dr. Watkins's support.

Caledonia, Rusk cty, Texas
November the 23rd 1862

My Dear Absent Husband,

I received your letter dated the 2nd on yesterday evening. It found us all well or at least nearly so. Jane has been ill all day today for the first day since she took sick. The rest well. I have no news of any importance to write you. The weather is about cool enough to be pleasant. We had about a weeks rain but it has been clear for several days and the most of the people are done sowing grain. We are about half done, I think. I came very near not sowing at home from the fact that old man Jones came in and said that he was very anxious to get the place back if you would let him have it on reasonable terms & I believed that you would do it if you were at home. I do not pretend to know what is best to do, but it seems to me that it would be better for us involved as we are & our debts are constantly increasing & we will not make a support I am afraid much less anything to pay our debts with. I am almost ready sometimes to tell Pa to let him have it without waiting for an answer from you for I think you would sanction it, that is if he will do right in the matter. He is coming to see me & I will then learn what he is willing to do in regard to it & will be better able to say what I think is best. Pa thinks it would be infinitely better for us as it would throw us out of debt & if you ever come back we can find another home somewhere else. I do not want you to infer from the above or anything that I shall say after this that it is only because I do not want to stay here alone that I want him to have it back but because I think it would be better for us for if the war should last only twelve months longer it will leave us in a very bad condition to pay our debts, if longer than that we would be stripped of half that we have. I would have to hire out the negroes but one. Pa thinks that he will have land enough for only about one of them & I had rather keep Tom & Charles if he had land. As it is can keep only one. I sometime think that I had better keep Tom as he is so hard headed & is just the age to take up with bad habits most readily & no person would watch him as I would not take the same interest in training him & Charlie is very small to hire out & if I could get Tom with the right sort of a man I had better do it on account of Charlie's size. I will want to keep both the women with me on account of their children. Jane wants to know before she goes back home & Pa don't want to make any arrangement until he could hear from you & that will take until about Christmas to hear from you & that much longer to hear from him again. It would be February before I would know what to do.

Nov the 25 As I did not finish my letter the other day I will now proceed again. We are still well, Jane improving also. I am more frustrated than ever now about what to do as how to proceed. I saw old man Jones yesterday & today also. He is pressing me & Pa to know what he may depend on. I do not know what to do or say in the matter or whether anything but from what I have often heard you say about it I am almost ready to say let it go on reasonable terms for I do not think that it is worth while for me to try to stay here without some one to stay with me for the negroes will not work & all the men up to forty are ordered into camps immediately & it will not leave a man below old man Stranges & there is constantly droves of negroes arriving from Mississippi, Louisiana, and Tennessee. They will overrun the country with them. I am fearful there is 75 or so at Johnsons, about that many at Dr. Ross'es so I hear but do not know whether or not there is as many as that. There is also a large drove at Mt. Enterprise. One of Uncle Wynne's brothers sent about fifty out from Holly Springs, Miss. So if there is no harm in them there will be no good from it. Old Mr. Jones says that he will do what is right about the place & I think that we had better let him have it if he will not that I feel myself capable of advising you in the matter but surrounded as I am by the most unfavorable circumstances I think it best to let it go. He also says that to wait to hear from you he will not be able to move back this winter & wants me to hold on another year but I told him if I left it would be this winter & if I had to stay here another year I did not intend to leave at all. I promised him this evening to send Pa word to come down & let them talk it over & come to some understanding about what they thought would be right & see how he would trade as I do not know yet what he is willing to do as he seems rather backward in talking about what he will do in the matter & if they should make any arrangement about it & you blame any one at all, blame me with it as I know that Pa had rather not take any action in this thing until he hears from you. Indeed he has said so but it appears to me that it is perfectly useless for me to undertake to stay here and there is not a man in the neighborhood that I could get to see to my business for me & you said in your letter of the 26 of Sept that if the men up to forty five were taken out of the country that was not willing for me to stay here & if I did leave you had rather let old man Jones have the place back than to leave & let it go rack. I would rather hear from you than to let him have it without. I could not think of such a thing if I had not heard you express yourself so often that way when you were at home & had rather endure anything that I can stand than to [do] what you would be dissatisfied with but I do not know what will be done or said. Old man Jones says that if they do not trade that they can agree on what they think is right & report to you & if they do make a bargain I suppose it will be left open for you to sanction. I believe so strong that I am almost ready to move some place for I am afraid that if I agree to it will be too late to make much towards leaving us the ground. I intend to start a team me & Pa between us. I will furnish three mules him one & wagon & driver & he says there could be money made [fold or break in paper] . . . make everything do something towards making a support which they will not make unless I will get someone to superintend for me. The weather is pretty cold this morning. I have my killing hogs up if I have some of the small ones that I am going to farm them out until I can see if I hire out. If I do ten of the largest will make me meat plenty. I am almost certain to loose some of my sows this winter as I have not a turnip for them nor nothing else but cotton seed but if they do die it will not be because I do not try to save them for I give my hogs, cows & sheep closer attention now than they ever had. I will try and get sent your coats by some of the men that are going back. If I can get them to take them. I am very lonesome these times. You know how I am about as well all I can tell you is if it were not for your kind letters which I receive pretty often I could not be as well satisfied as I am. Indeed I would be almost crazy & have received eleven letters from you. I will write very regular & often so if you do not get the letters it will not be my fault. Cotton cards are thirty dollar pair. Bogess went to Miss. & got a woman to go into Memphis & get some. He sold an hundred pair out by eleven o'clock & could have sold many more. I heard that there had some money come from the [unreadable] to you but do not know how much. I will hold on to it until I hear from you. I have bought five lbs of tobacco for you. Is that enough?

From Your Loving Wife
NF Whatley

NOVEMBER 24, 1862
WJW TO NFW

"There have been a good many deaths lately . . . The tenth anniversary of our wedding day . . . It is a time we often reflect back to as being the happiest of our lives."

On the march to Arkansas Post . . . Guaranteed a fight . . . No mail in two weeks . . . More deaths in camp.

Little Rock Arkansas
November 24th 1862

My Dear Wife,

I just have a few moments this morning to drop you a line to let you know [where] we are and the condition of affairs. We landed here Saturday evening, and will leave here in thirty minutes for the Arkansas Post, about 100 miles below here by water. The boats are now at the wharf and we are packing our baggage as fast as we can. Gen Holmes has just been round at our inspection and told us that the enemy were there and that we would get into a fight and be sure to whip them. I received a letter from Jane Saturday which informed me that you were well but had several cases of measles among the negroes. I answered that letter immediately. I would be very glad to have had a letter from you before I left here as I have not had one in over two weeks. Our boys are in very good health and spirits, but there have been a good many deaths lately. We lost another man out of our company died three days ago (Calvin R. Price). You recollect he was at our house with old man Jack a few years ago. I have not got any more clothing since Colley came in and I reckon now I will stand a pretty good chance to lose them as we are now not in reach of Roberts regiment. I don't think we will stay at the Post long. The object is I think to fight and return somewhere in this section. I may get a letter from you yet before we leave as the courier has gone for the mail. I write this hurriedly to let you know where I am going. You must continue to write to me and direct your letters as before until you are otherwise directed. You must be of good cheer, take good care of yourself and children. Send my best respects to Mr. Miller and family. Tell him I am much obliged to him for taking hold of your business for you, and assisting you in my absence. I sent to Searcy to get you some cards, but could not buy them with confederate money at any price. I have written to you every week and will continue to do so every chance I have. I would be very glad to hear from you a little oftener, but I will not grumble for perhaps you write and I fail to receive. It is with much pleasure that I write to you on this, the tenth anniversary of our wedding day. It is a time that we often reflect back to as being the happiest of our lives, and I have doubt but you will write to me today, and are perhaps writing to me now at this hour, ten o'clock A.M. They are issuing knapsacks and haversacks for the companies and I judge when we land that we will have to carry our baggage on our backs which will be pretty heavy on some of the boys for some of them. I have just received a precious letter from you written on the 9th inst. Which was the same date of Jane's but gave me great satisfaction. You must excuse brevity this time and read the best you can for we are now advised to fall into lines. Now my dear wife and children fare well for the present.

May God bless you.
From your love,
WJ Whatley

DECEMBER 1862

"I often think of my little children and sometimes fear that they . . .
will perhaps never have the same attachment for me they once had."

*Taylor's regiment and WJW move by boat from Little Rock to Arkansas Post . . .
A stop at Pine Bluff . . . Drunkenness on board . . . Teetotaler WJW reflects on
leadership, whiskey, and abstinence . . . Urges NFW to write . . . Dreams of
her . . . Will his children know him? . . . Writes to his father in Alabama . . .
Concern about the stock, especially the hogs . . . Martin will care for the hogs.*

Camp Near Arkansas Post
December 1st 1862

My dear wife

Eight days ago to day I wrote to you from Little Rock, and stated to
you that we would take a boat for this place in thirty minutes from
the time I was writing. We were then loading the boat but did not get
off until the next morning about nine o'clock when we started aboard
the Julia Roane, and landed here Friday morning about 9 a.m. The
river was dug low and we could not travel at night which caused us
to be three days getting there and we were then two days ahead of
the rest of our brigade for some of them arrived in last night. They

were on large side wheel Steamers and run onto several sand bars which delayed them considerably. The river is very crooked and full of logs and sand bars. I can give but little idea of the distances we traveled from my own observation, but I believe they call it two hundred and forty miles by water, but it is not more than half that distance by land. We had a very disagreeable trip. The boat was very much crowded and all on deck and the weather quite cold on the river. We came down to Pine Bluffs and landed about three hours and had quite a jollification, the boys found some good old (how could you so [colloquialism referring to aged whiskey]) at only ten dollars a quart and I think in two hours time there was fifty drunk men on board and as many more in a good lively humor what you might call gentlemanly tight. For my part I got as drunk as I ever want to be just by looking at the balance without taking a drop myself. I have got to take my first drink yet, and experience has taught me that I am better off without it, and I expect to return home to you, without taking any of the foul stuff which only makes a man drunk and a fool and destroys his health and unfits him for business. Our col [colonel] fortunately was sober and has had all the officers who were drunk under arrest ever since we have been here which seems to consume of them very much and I hope it may be the means of keeping them sober in future, for if there is any thing I do abhor it is drunkenness especially in men who are in prominent positions, for we have too much at stake in this matter to be ruled and governed by drunk men. I saw some men drunk that day I never saw drunk before. But I believe the rule will hold good, that if a man drinks at all he is liable to drink too much. I have seen Hiram May & John Terrell here. They belong to Gillespies regiment. May will start home in a few days, and I will send this letter by him if I don't get an opportunity sooner, but I reckon our mail will be sent off tomorrow and if so I will send this there and write to you again by then if I have any news to write you. I have succeeded in getting a quire [twenty-five sheets] of paper lately and a supply of envelopes which fits me properly for writing to you, and you may expect letters regular, and recollect darling that I keep you accountable to answer them. For I left you a plenty of paper and will expect you to keep it for the express purpose of writing to me, for you know I do love to get a letter from you and hear from my little pets. Yesterday was warm and cloudy nearly all day and last night we had a good shower of rain. I went to bed and sleep while it was raining and dreamed of my darling safe at home. I thought I was with you and enjoying myself as in days of yore and felt perfectly happy. But when I awoke and found that I was mistaken and instead of being at home I was in the Arkansas swamp my hopes were all blasted. But the time is coming I do believe when I will be permitted to return to you again and hold you once more to my bosom where you can rest in peace and live in the full enjoyment of connubial bliss. I often think of my little children and sometimes fear that they will become in a great measure weaned from me, and will perhaps never have the same attachment for me they once had, children you know are not like grown people. They can easily forget and take up with any new thing that comes along. I know that I will find you always the same, and I intend to be as true to you as I know thou art to me. You know little Jane has even been troubled with a cough and I dread the consequences of her having measles, but I know you will take all the care of her that you possibly can and I submit you all into the hands of our heavenly father, who will protect you from all harm. I never lay my head on my pillow to sleep without thinking of you all and asking his blessing upon you. I hope you will all get along well and keep good health. You will not have to have the measles but once and I know your ma will assist you all she can and let Jane stay with you as much as she can. I am sorry to hear that Jesses health is so bad and think if I was in his place I would not go into the service anymore before spring unless I regained my health and got stout again, for I dread the winter here very much. A great deal of it is fatal. I wrote a letter to my father [Seaborn Jane Thornton Whatley, Calhoun County, Alabama] a few days ago since informing him of my where abouts and giving him in detail the condition of matters at home as nigh as I knew them I know that he will be a friend to you if you should ever need it. But I do hope you will get along well, and have good health and not suffer for any of the necessarys of life. If you are deprived of some of the luxuries I learn that you are all still hard run for cotton cards and will consequently have a hard time making clothes but I hope you will continue to have a good resolution and succeed in keeping clothes plenty. I wrote to you sometime since to send me my other jeans & rubber coat if you had an opportunity. I would like very well to have both but if you can only get a chance to send the overcoat, as I can make out to wear the one I have but it is too light and if I had that one I know I could dispose of the one I have. Harlon Woodum left there about the 10th of August for clothing for the regiment, and I suppose from some letters I have lately seen from Texas that some of the people there are not advised up to this date that he is in Texas or that any one had been sent for clothing for this regiment. A large majority of the regiment have a very contemptible opinion of him. James Walker was over and stayed all night with me last Sunday night. He is in very good health. I don't visit other regiments but very little as we are now denied that privilege and if we go we either have to slip out of the guard line or make application to three different offices for a pass and have them all to sign it, which they frequently refuse to do, and for my part I prefer to stay in my company than make any such application. You must keep me well posted about matters at home. You must have your hogs attended to, marked regularly, and see that none of them are lost or go wild if you have good mast.[1] Mr. Martin must attend to my John's hogs if he has not done it. I would like to know how much corn you have made. Peas, potatoes and to be kept and dried from time to time of what you have done and how you are getting along generally, for I would greatly prefer hearing about you and yours than any thing else that can or may transpire in that country. If you have plenty of turnips you must not let your stock suffer for you know that they will keep them fat and yield a fine chance of milk and butter is worth here a dollar a pound. You must send me some tobacco. It is worth here two dollars a plug which will nearly take the whole of infantry wages, and I suppose we will only draw that from the time we were dismounted. You must read my letters to the children and tell them I want them to be good boys and girls and obedient unto you. I never lay my head on my pillow that I don't think of you and ask god to be merciful unto you. I will write to you again when I get your next letter. And if we should leave here sooner I will advise you of the fact though I suppose you get the Little Rock paper. Give my love to your pa, family, and all other relations and tell them I would be glad to have a letter from any of them at any time. Write soon to your affectionate husband.

W. J. Whatley

1. For "mast years," see Wohlleben's *The Hidden Life of Trees,* 19–21.

DECEMBER 4, 1862
WJW TO NFW

"I believe the biggest half of our stay here is about something to eat and the other part is about wives and sweethearts. . . . I submit you all in the hands of our heavenly father who will protect from all harm."

Misery of Arkansas Post . . . The Confederates are trapped . . . Rain and pneumonia . . . Winter quarters . . . Food and appetite . . . Wives' and sweethearts' talk . . . Yearning for NFW . . . Take care of little Jane.

Arkansas Post, Ark[1]
December 4th 1862

My Dear Wife,

I write to you from this place the 1st inst, four days ago but as Mr. Harper will start from here for Texas [Henderson] tomorrow I will write to you again knowing that you are always anxious to hear from me and to know my whereabouts and condition of my health which is about all I have at the present time to communicate to you. We are still here in camp in one of the wettest and muddiest places you can conceive of. Our waggons landed here last evening but are on the opposite side of the river from us, and the arrangement for crossing the river is very bad, and it will take them several days to get over, and when they get here I suppose we will move a mile or two from this place and go into winter quarters. It has been raining a slow rain nearly ever since we have been here which has made our encampment very sloppy. There is considerable sickness here now, and it is increasing daily. Doctor Smith told me yesterday that he had seven cases of pneumonia and several others that he thought would soon develop themselves, and thinks there will be a great deal of sickness here if we don't leave here soon. When I wrote to you last I had heard no talk of winter quarters, but our Col says we are going into them and I reckon there is no doubt of it. I am told that the balance of the division (except our brigade) are going into quarters up in a few miles of Brownsville, where we were dismounted last summer. So we will be so far from them that there can be little or no communication with them. I have not seen Jimmy Walker in two or three weeks and consequently don't know anything about him. My health is as good as usual, but think if we don't all have pneumonia here it will not be for want of a good chance. Colley is in fine health, went out hunting yesterday with two or three others and brought in two deer and two fine turkeys and you ought to have been here this morning to have seen me frying steaks (of which you know I am very fond). At dinner we had roast turkey and a fine venison stew which has put us all in good humor and made us nearly fat. It would astonish you to be here and see us eat. I don't believe I was ever so hearty in my life. I believe the biggest half of our stay here is about something to eat and the other part is about wives and sweethearts. The boys all say they are going to marry when they get home. Friend Colley sends his best respects to Lex and Preshie and says tell Preshie that he will write to her soon according to promise. We are now on the east side of the Arkansas river about one mile from the Post which is the oldest settled place in the state. We have some very strong fortifications here (that is they are said to be) I have not seen them myself only at a distance, for I don't think they permit anyone to go into the fort except officers of high rank. They have been making preparations here for a fight for some time. There are about four thousand members besides our brigade, and our entire division to be here soon, and will be here doubtless if we have a fight, but I think it is uncertain about that, though I am told that the fed pickets have been in four miles of here and the gun boats in about twelve. We are about fifty miles from the Mississippi river by water, and about ten or twelve miles from the White river and in a very flat low country and some of the richest land I ever saw, and the boy's say that it abounds in game. Colley and some of the other boy's have gone out hunting today and I reckon if they are lucky we will have some venison tomorrow. Patrick brought us in a fine opossum yesterday which boy's have on baking now with a fine chance of potatoes around him, which will give mess [unreadable] a fine dinner. I find Gillespies and Wilkes regiments here (two of Carter's old brigade)[2] they have been here about three months and are now going into winter quarters. Some of them have their cabins up and they look very snug. They are about fourteen feet square and daubed close which makes them very comfortable. I don't know how long we will remain here, but I hope we will not stay here long. We will have a great deal of sickness. General Holmes says that we will not go into winter quarters and I reckon we will leave here as soon as all probability of a fight passes away. I would not be surprised now at anything. We may be sent over the Mississippi or we may go back up the river or remain here, but if we leave here soon we will have to walk for at the present state of the river we cannot go back on boats. There is some sickness still with us and always will be I reckon but no deaths in our regiment since we left Camp Nelson, unless it has been among those we left at the hospital. My health is as good as usual have had no chill now in over two weeks and weigh a hundred and seventy four pounds which is more than I ever weighed before. After dinner I have just dined on opossum had a fine dinner and feel considerably better. I have done written you all the news that I have but will fill up my space. We are now drawing our beef and meal [cornmeal] as usual but our beef is much better than it was some time back and we are dining very well. I believe that I love beef more than I ever did in my life. We get some sugar and molasses occasionally which answers for a dessert. I wrote to you some time since for you to send me your likeness if you could conveniently see an artist and have an opportunity of sending it. I would like very much to have it. Take care of my gun and don't let it rust, for I will need it when I come home. Our company have all drawed guns who did not have them, and the most of us have muskets which are about as good as any for yankee hunting. The weather is considerably cooler today than yesterday. It has been cloudy all day and I don't think the weather is settled yet. I fear we will have more falling weather which we are very illy prepared for, for we have not more than half tents enough and a great many of them are very inferior. I am very glad you have got Mr. Miller to see to business for you. I know he will do you justice tell him I want him to control the negroes and if any of them prove refractory to take them down and straighten them. We are obliged to make something at home and it will not do to put up with the negroes laziness, if they won't go ahead and work they must be made to it, and if they don't work they will be an expense. Take notice I leave the business all in your hands and whatever you do will be right with me, and I want you to have the negroes controlled and made to work. Your pa will advise with you and assist you all he can, it is impossible for me to be of such benifit to you for I am clear away and I get your letters very unregular which will prevent me from knowing the condition of your affairs until too late to advise you. I hope however you will write to me and keep me posted as well as you can about matters at home, for I have a great interest here in fact all my interest is now in your hands. Take good care of my little ones for they lie very nigh my heart, it is for their sake and yours that I am here and in a measure contented to stay and battle for your rights and hope there is a brighter day dawning upon us and ere long we will be permitted to return home more than conquerors and again enjoy our own domestic happiness. You must take care of your paper and write to me whenever you can get a chance for I will always be glad to hear from you. We are here on the Arkansas river at

Arkansas Post in Arkansas county and Arkansas State so you see it is Arkansas all over and for my part I am getting tired of Arkansas. The boys are writing home now, today is leisure with us as we have had no drilling to do since we came here yet, and have not had out as strong a guard as heretofore, but I reckon we will have it out soon. We have all drawn nap sacks and are now properly prepared for carrying our baggage and I fear we will have to go at it soon. Our wagons have not got here yet, but they will be here I reckon before we leave for it will be impossible for us to carry all our things. You will still direct your letters to Little Rock as before and write to me as soon as you receive this and let me know how you are getting along. Tell cousin Syl that I shall expect that letter from him and hope he will not disappoint me. I would be glad to write to him and a good many others but it takes about all my leisure time in writing you. We have no tables here and you must make allowances for all the ill shaped letters you see. I am writing with my nap sack in my lap sitting on a sheep skin in the fashion of a taylor on his bench which is about as good a position as I can get in. Give my love to cousin Haden & family when you see them tell the girls they might write to me. I would be glad to hear from them. Tell my little boys & girls I have not forgotten them and they must remember their pa and be good children and mind their ma. I wish the boys could be at school. I will close by subscribing my self your true and devoted husband.

W. J. Whatley

1. Arkansas Post is an ancient site located in the Bayou Country. Since 1689 and La Salle, Arkansas Post on the Arkansas River has had at least four locations, two French and two Spanish, the last of which was turned over by the Spanish to the United States in 1804. Arkansas Post lost out to Little Rock as the location for Arkansas' capital.

2. To read more about Carter's brigade, see Anne J. Bailey and Bruce Allardice, "Carter, George Washington," *Handbook of Texas Online,* accessed May 29, 2018. http://www.tshaonline.org/handbook/online/articles/fca70.

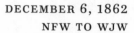

"Christmas is close at hand & my poor husband is so far away."

Rumors of troop movements . . . Vicksburg . . . Preparations for moving and selling the place . . . Their slaves get shoes . . . News of Jane . . . John goes to school, can spell . . . Efforts to keep WJW's memory before the children . . . Bleak Christmas ahead . . . Separation . . . Dreams of him.

December the 6th at Caledonia, Rusk, Texas

My beloved husband, I seat myself this morning to drop you a few lines. This leaves us all well with the exception of colds. I would have written to you several days ago but heard that there had A brigade been ordered to some point on the Miss river probably Vicksburg & that Taylors was one of the regs [regiments]. But I was up at Pa's yesterday & he told me that the order had been countermanded. I am now fixing to move up to Pa's. The negroes will go up today to build some cabins as there are none at the houses. I have sold my corn down here & have bought up there & that will save me a great deal of trouble. Dr. Attaway has rented the land and a Mr. Young has rented the houses. The Dr. pitched right after the place as soon as he heard that old man Jones had got it back. He offered six dollars per acre but he could not get it. Mr. Jones wants you [to] send a power of attorney to sell it. He prefers that to having a deed written & sending it there for you to sign and it will also leave the thing open so he can have the deed made to whom he pleases. We are now having some very cold weather, had a very late frost last night, the first white frost that we have had this winter. It is very cold this morning. I have just got my negroes shoes. They all have shoes now from Tillis. Mr. Treadwell made up some of the meanest leather that I ever saw in my life. I sent it to a regular tanner & had it worked over or they never could have worn it. Jane says that she is going to feed the chickens & turkeys for her Pa. She is sitting down by me now talking as fast as she can chatter. She daily talks about her Pa who is so far from us. John is a very great comfort to me. In fact if it were not for my little children I would be the most miserable being separated as I am from him I love the best of all the world. John has been up at his grandpa's for three weeks. I brought him home yesterday. He went to school all the time. He can spell in words of four letters pretty well. Mary is here, there & everywhere. She is a perfect romp & as lively as a cricket. She can say "O, Pa" very plain but poor little sweet child I do not know whether she will ever see you again or not or whether she can recollect anything about you or not. I try to keep her from forgetting you by telling her about her Pa. I will move up to Pa's [Dr. Watkins] in about two weeks. Christmas is close at hand & my poor husband is so far away from me that it will not be as pleasant a Christmas as the preceding ones by a great deal. For I do not care how pleasantly I am situated I cannot be happy without my dear husband who is so much dearer to me than all the world besides but I will not grumble for I know that you have to undergo so much more than any of us that I will try to be satisfied & will be thankful if you can be spared to come back to your family who I know thinks as much of you as anyone can think of a father & husband. I frequently dream of you [for WJW's dreams, see WJW to NFW, December 4, 1862]. I dreamed the other night that you were at home but alas for me it is not a reality. If you can only keep well I will endeavor to keep in good spirits. But when I hear that you are sick it appears to me that it is more than I can stand. It is now three months and over since you left home the last time & I do not know when you will ever come back to us again, but I do hope & pray that you will be spared to come back when this war closes if not before. I will do the best that I can. I will write to you every week unless I get so scarce of paper then it will be better to write not so often so you may hear from us once in a while as that will be better than not at all. I still have plenty of paper & I think I can get some from Anne [Paisley] as she has a book that is not much used out of. You must write often as I want to hear every week. The last letter of yours was written the ninth of last month. Write when you get this & remember that this is from your affectionate wife,

N. F. Whatley

DECEMBER 8, 1862
WJW TO NFW

"You must do the best you can and I will come home when I can."

Arkansas Post's conditions deteriorate . . . News of the Alabama Whatleys, their service and losses . . . Business advice on disposing of their place . . . Uncertainty of the mails . . . Urgent need for winter clothing . . . No possibility of an exemption or furlough . . . Rumors of a Virginia victory.

(Write to Little Rock)
Arkansas Post Arkansas
December the 8th 1862

My Dear Wife,

Your kind letter of the 21st of November came to hand a few moments ago, and it is with great haste that I seat myself to reply. My health is good I believe as good as it ever was in my life, but we are in a very low locality and have considerable sickness in camps and fear there will be more if we don't move from here soon. But when we do move I reckon it will not be far, for I think we will go into winter quarters in this place. I have no news to write to you for I wrote to you just a week ago, and nothing of interest has transpired since. I received two letters from Alabama a few days since, one from pa and one from Sister Mollie. They stated that my relations were all well who were at home but the most of them were in the army. Bro Seaborn and James are in Virginia and have been in ten or twelve fights. My uncle George who was with them (and who I wrote to you sometime since was dead) has been wounded three times and is now a prisoner, and father did not know whether he was dead or alive, but he has some hope that he is living.[1] In his letter he sends his love to you and children and Aunt Mary [Strong]. I received a letter from your Pa a few days since informing me that Parson Jones was in, and would probably like to buy the place back in case I wished to sell. I have just answered his letter and instructed him to let him have the place back by paying back the money I had paid him and giving up my note. I did not know what else to do for it seems to be impossible to make any management at home that will do to depend upon, as Mr. Miller now has to leave you. I know of no other chance to get anyone to assist you, and you are too far from your Pa for him to help you much. I hope you will be satisfied with the arrangement as I think under existing circumstances it is the best we can do. Your Pa wrote to me that he would move you to his Elliott place and do the best he could for you, in case I should sell you would then be where you can be protected and have company and someone to assist you to get along with your affairs which would take a great load off of my mind. It is beyond the power of any of us to tell anything about when the war will close, and if I have to be separated from you I want you to be where you can have some satisfaction. I have written to Mr. Jones also and made the same proposition to him and instructed him if he wanted to take the trade to apply to your Pa who I have given full instructions to about it. In case he does not want the place, you and your pa can do what you think is best. If you wish to move from your house you can do so or any other way you think is best. I will look for Mr. Miller in a few days. Ed Elliott got in on the fifth last and said he and others were fixing to start back to their respective commands. Your letter was in answer to mine of the 31st of October. You ought to have had two or three letters from me than that, and I know that you don't get all my letters from the way you write. I got a letter from you about the last of Oct in which you stated you would send me some clothing when Thad's came, and I understand that the waggon that brought his left home on the 9th of Nov and is now at Roberts regiment about sixty or seventy miles above here, so it seems from that that you did not avail yourself of that opportunity. I was expecting them by that wagon and one of our company is gone up there now to see about them and other clothing that is there for the regiment. If you have not sent them yet, you will please send them by the first opportunity as I am very much in need of my coats. The one I have is too small, and I have no overcoat at all. I have socks a plenty to do six months. I got two more pair when I came back that I left with my mess last summer which has helped me out. You need not trouble yourself to send me my tobacco for if you have it to buy there, I had as well buy it here. I have about worn out one pair of my pants and would not object to having another pair if you have them but if I can get them in a month or two, it will answer. If I had my long drawers I would use them but am not particular about them and you had better not send them unless you can get them here very soon for I will not want to be troubled with them next summer. So you will be sure and send my coats the first chance and send me a pair of pants when you get them ready and the drawers if you can get them here soon. I am glad to hear that my little daughter has recovered her health. May the lord keep her and the rest of you in my absence and save your lives and health until I return. I am always glad to get a letter from you for it is the nearest I can come to seeing you and talking with you. I will not fail to write to you once a week if I can get a chance, but I fear our mails will be uncertain here this winter for it will have to be carried about a hundred miles over a very low country. You spoke something about the exemption law in your letter. I think that only applies to men who are out of the service. So I don't think there is much chance. You must do the best you can and I will come home when I can. I don't think there will be any furloughs this winter, for we are where we will be expecting a fight and none will be apt to get home. But I don't much think we will have a fight soon, and it seems that we will never do anything but lie and wallow around [next few words unreadable]. We have had another big fight in Virginia and give the worst whipping we have ever gave them yet, but we have no particulars and consequently it will not do to rely upon. Maj. Noble has been promoted to Lieut. Col. And Capt Tucker is now our Major. We are getting plenty of beef and bread and doing very well. Your acquaintances and kin are all in good health and fine spirits. It is getting dark and I must close. The mail is going out in the morning. Give my love to my dear little children and tell them that I love them dearly. My best respects to all enquiring friends. Write to me as soon as you get this and let me have all the news. I hope you will be satisfied about the land trade. I know you are willing for me to act for you, and I think that is best.

> Your dear husband
> W. J. Whatley

1. His Uncle George, reported wounded several times at Antietam and taken prisoner, actually died there; Seaborn and James were accurately reported as alive at that time. James was killed later, and Seaborn survived the war.

DECEMBER 13, 1862
WJW TO NFW

"My country . . . bleeding at every pore, and calling men. . . .
He that is not willing to fight for his country is not worthy to
live in a free and independent government."

Worried about Jane . . . Separation agonies . . . Patriotic musings . . . Health concerns . . . Camp moved to higher ground . . . War weariness . . . More about selling their place . . . Much advice about selling out . . . Importance of NFW's father . . . Complex debts . . . Wants the boys to go to school . . . Wants a "good report" on the "negroes."

My dear beloved wife,

Your letter of the 25th of Nov came to hand yesterday and reached me last night out on picket guard. I am truly glad to hear you are all well and hope by this time my little daughter has entirely recovered her health and again has her countenance lit up with a lovely smile and can lisp the oft called name of Pa. It would do me more good than anything on earth to see you and my children and have the pleasure of spending some time with you. I never knew what it was to be separated from you before this horrible war broke out, but such is fate. I am here and have as much right to be here perhaps as anyone else, and I hope I feel as great an interest in my country which is now bleeding at every pore, and calling men into the field continually to defend her against an invading foe and he that is not willing to fight for his country is not worthy to live in a free and independent government. My health is as good as ever but not so with the boy's generally, for we have considerable sickness here, have had a good deal of wet weather lately, and it was impossible to keep dry. Some are dying daily. One of my mess L.B.C. Pullaway is quite sick, taken last night and I am somewhat uneasey about him, but hope with good care that he will be up again soon. We have moved about a mile and a half down the river from where we first stopped here and have a little higher and better situation. We have not done anything yet towards building but will go at it in a day or two. But we are so poorly supplied with tools that I fear it will be after Christmas before we get them ready to go into. One brigade now have their cabins up, and I think it looks like the largest negro quarters I ever saw in my life. [next ten or so words unreadable] They are daubed so tightly that I fear the consequences of taking cold when we have to leave them, and there is no telling about how soon we may have it to do, for frequently when we make the largest preparations to stay at a place we leave it sooner than any other. It is impossible to tell anything about this war. I have thought it would close next spring, but I see no better prospect now than there was several months ago, and I fear that if it don't close by that time that it will become desperate and we will have a life and death struggle for liberty & rights. In regard to selling our place, I will say that your notions accord with mine, and it will meet with my full approbation for you to let the old man have it back if he will do right. I have already written to you and your Pa knows about it and gave full instructions about it, but I will state the terms here for fear that the other letters may be delayed. I write to your Pa to let him have the place back by paying back the money I had paid him. I wrote to old man Jones at his own post office and made the same proposition to him. You were right in refusing to keep the place another year, for if you have to remain [at] the place another year we will not let him have it at all, for it is more for your satisfaction than anything else that I would sell. If you do sell, you had better go up near your pa and you and him make the best arrangement you can with our little [ones]. I think it best to keep the negroes with you. If you can make any arrangement to get land convenient enough to work for provisions are going to be very high, and if you don't make plenty at home you will have to buy which will cost you enormously. If you could rent land enough to work and your Pa is willing to do so I would rather you would let him take your force and work with his and give you a proportionate part of what is made. But if it cannot be done and you have them to attend to perhaps you had better hire out all but what your pa has land to work. If you can get good wages you are right in keeping the women with you on account of their children. You and your Pa can arrange that to your own notion for I know he will advise you for the best if he knows it. I have every confidence in him, as you know before and had as soon leave you under his care as my own father. You must do the best you can with your stock and if you do move try & not loose any of your hogs, for they are now the most valuable stock you have. I paid a few days ago thirty ct a pound for four lbs of pork, and you may judge from that that we don't eat much hog meat there, but we had a fine pot of hominy for breakfast and dinner and enough left for supper. If Matt or Wm Hopson have sent me any money, you had better get your Pa to attend to it for you and let him enter credits of the amts they wish to pay on their notes. You will find them with my other papers in my note pocket, and then you had better take up my notes as far as you have money. If you don't make the land trade you had better pay it all on the land note, but if you make that trade you can pay our other debts. First, let your Pa have enough to pay what we owe him if he will take and I reckon he can use it so as to make it answer his purpose. I owe Dr. Attaway a note & Johnson has a note twenty or twenty five dollars, a small note to Kings estate $5 & 85 cts to Taylor's estate, and account with Ed Hamlett and other debts you may have contracted since I have been from home. If [unreadable] has got his cotton he and Barthold are paid for last year which is all the debts I have out except what I am owing Thad and if you get money enough I want every dollar settled that I owe. I had forgotten a small debt I owed Jim Easley of two dollars and a quarter for some peas which I want you to pay over to his widow. I want you if you move to send the little boys to school if you can have any opportunity. They are now suffering for school-ing, John especially. He will soon be eight years old, and tell them they must learn fast that I may hear them read when I come home. I see from a letter from Wm Young to Doc that you have paid them a visit last fall. I am glad you did so. I know my old aunt was glad to see you. She is an exception and has had her share of trouble. [Un-readable] regiment is now at Port Hudson, about fifty miles above New Orleans.[1] Ed Strong [WJW's cousin] is in fine health. I have a letter a few days since from one of the company. I hope to hear soon that Jessee has recovered his health and strength sufficiently to re-turn home where he had better stay through the winter if he can. I would be very glad to know that your Sister had got in good health. (There is no better girl than Jane) As for news I have nothing of any importance to write for nothing has transpired here worth relating and to write you what I hear would be to fill up a letter with stuff. I hope therefore you will not complain at the length of this letter for I have now pened [penned] everything that I have to write. I will send this letter by Billy Loyd who [has] gone up with his brother to take his horse back. He will leave in the morning for home. If you have to hire out any of the negroes tell them they must behave themselves and let me hear a good report of them. You acknowledge the receipt of seven letters up to the 2nd of last month. I have received eight from you up to the present, and hope to get another soon. I would like to hear from all my friends but I reckon paper is too scarce. Write to Little Rock as before and give me all the news. I love to hear from you and hear how you are getting along. I will write to you again soon. Kiss my children for me and read them my letters,

> from your absent husband
> W. J. Whatley

December 14th I open this letter to write a few lines in answer to a letter I read from you per this morning in relation to the land trade with Old Man Jones. He wrote that he [Dr. Watkins] had let him have the place, subject to my approval which is entirely satisfactory with me and will sign it over to him when he sends a deed. You can then sign it and your Pa can fix all up, am glad that you can now have some satisfaction and I hope you will get along well and make plenty. I will write to you soon.

> My love to all yours as ever.
> W. J. Whatley

1. Port Hudson, Louisiana: Besieged for forty-eight days, Confederate forces there surrendered July 9, 1863, after receiving confirmation of Vicksburg's July 4 surrender.

DECEMBER 18, 1862
WJW TO NFW

"The darkest hour is just before day, and I am in hopes that we may have peace yet, soon. If it was not for hope we would all go under."

WJW in good shape . . . His comrades dying in camp . . . Defensive prepara-
tions . . . Anxiety about Vicksburg . . . Advises her about moving livestock . . .
Keep the livestock—particularly the hogs . . . Hogs preferable to Confederate
money . . . Pay their debts out of cotton sale . . . The men are deeply home-
sick . . . Hopes for peace.

Arkansas Post Arkansas
December 18th 1862

Dear Wife,

I seat myself this morning to respond to your's of the 29th of Nov and
also the 1st Dec [these letters didn't survive], both of which came to
hand last night, and found me in the enjoyment of good health and
strength and able to do any duty as a soldier which is pretty light
now, as we have commenced putting up our cabins and are on duty
every other day. But if I can keep well and stout I will not mind it.
There is still considerable sickness here and some few are dying.
We lost another man out of our company on the 8th inst (Wm. Robertson) he died at the hospital at Camp Nelson, was left there sick
when we left that place. He is a son of old John Robertson who lived
near Aunt Mary Strong a few years ago. He is the 4th man that has
died out of Company F since I came back in the summer, making 12
in all. We have only two men now at the hospital and they are both
improving and will be well soon if they have no back set [setback].
We are under General Churchill's command and I reckon are entirely
cut loose from McCulloch as I learn that he is gone with the army to
reinforce Hindman up about Fort Smith. Hindman has had a fight
[Battle of Prairie Grove] up there recently and I suppose has had to
retreat, but was successful on the 1st day's fight, killing about twelve
hundred of the enemy. But I have seen no account of it and only tell
it as I have heard it. It is also reported that we have captured one
of Lincoln's best gun boats down about the mouth of the river. We
are making pretty extensive preparations here to receive the enemy whenever they may deem it proper or prudent to pay us a visit.

We have a very strong fort [Hindman] covered with iron and three very long guns mounted besides a number of small ones, and have out a long entrenchment for rifle pits with a canon mounted every eighty yards to prevent them from bringing up their land force, and it is said here that they can't approach us from any other direction when the river gets up high enough to bring up gun boats. We have had heavy rain lately and has swelled the river four or five feet, but it will soon run down. I don't look for any permanent rise before Spring. They are now expecting a battle at Vicksburg soon. There has been some talk our being ordered there and it may be done yet, but as we are now gone to building, we have got somewhat reconciled about it, for I assure that we have an aversion to taking that trip on foot as late in the season as this. I do hope and pray that our forces will be successful in that engagement for I think there is a great deal depending on it. Vicksburg is now the only hold we have and if we should loose that point they will have full possession of the Mississippi, and thereby completely divide the Confederate states and cut off all communications from one side to the other.[1] I was very glad to hear that you were all well for nothing on earth affords me so much pleasure as to hear from you and to hear that you are in good health, and now that you have sold out and will soon get near your Pa I hope you will get along better and be satisfied at least as well as you can under the circumstances. I am glad you have let the old man have the place back. We have lost by the operation but still I think it was best to let it go for I was not willing for you to stay there any longer unless you could have got someone to attend to business for you which is an impossibility at this time. You must try to get your stock all moved and take the best care of them you can. Have your calves all marked and branded before you leave, if you have not done it, that you may not loose them for if you leave them somewhere you are they may scatter and you will stand a chance to loose some of them. I think however if you think you can give them any attention you had better move them, or if you can get anyone to give them any attention you might leave the strongest of them until next Spring. I would prefer not to sell any of them as I had rather have stock than

Confederate money. Take good care of your hogs for if you have to buy meat it will cost you heavy. You had better make the negroes gather up all the old wood about the place for they will be useful about your place. I think if you can make any arrangement you had better keep all the negroes at home, for I fear they will live long and as provisions are sure to be high you had better make it at home if you can. However your Pa will do the best he can which will satisfy me, and I only make these statements in answer to your requests. You did right in paying Johnson though he did not pay you enough for your cotton, and I want you if you have the money to spare to pay every debt I owe and stop the interest. I will be able to get along very well on what I am making here, and if we should get cavalry pay I would have something to spare. We have never drew any more money, and the talk is now again that we will draw cavalry wages but it is uncertain. Our officers all drew money last week, which the privates were dissatisfied with but could not help themselves. The boys are getting quite anxious to get home and some say they are coming home at the end of twelve months whether they get a furlough or not, but I don't think any of them will do it unless they are furloughed and there is not much probability of getting them but the darkest hour is just before day, and I am in hopes that we may have peace yet, soon. If it was not for hope we would all go under. I received a letter from cousin Syl yesterday but it had been written a long time. You can tell him I have not seen Jimmy since I left Camp Nelson, and I suppose he has gone now with the balance [of] McCullough's army, and I can't tell when I will see him again. I tried to make a swap and get him into our company but failed to do so. If we were together now I think I could arrange it as Ed Elliott would like to get with his brother in that regiment. Tell John that I have got another gun that Jeff Davis gave me. It is an old musket with a bayonet on the end and can shoot Yankees and stick them too. Tell him he must [go] to school and learn fast and not let Arch beat him. I am glad to hear that he is learning and well pleased with school. I will bring them a present when I come home. I would like to be with you and eat your fat turkey, for I am fearful that we will not have any

Christmas dinner here, and I believe the boys have put it up that they will have to go without even an egg nog. We have to pay very dear for everything we get to eat, outside of our rations, which consists of beef and bread. I was sorry to hear that [Lorie] had lost her babe and sympathize with her in her bereavement. When you see her tender her my best love and wishes for her welfare. I will write to you once a week as I have done and try and keep you advised about matters and things here. You must excuse my short letter for I have written everything I can think of. Write soon and direct to Little Rock.

Your Husband in love
W. J. Whatley

1. William's comment about Vicksburg shows that he had an excellent grasp of the big picture. See account of the campaign by Terrence J. Winschel, a recently retired chief historian of Vicksburg National Military Park, https://www.battlefields.org/learn/articles/vicksburg.

DECEMBER 18, 1862
NFW TO WJW

"Since I have been sick I have taken several big cries. . . .
I frequently anticipate that happy hour when I can . . . sit on
your knee and be nestled in your arms."

NFW ill . . . Her most passionate letter . . . Declaration of her love for WJW . . . Dreams . . . Wants to send him a cake . . . No flour . . . Will send him pants, socks, five pounds of tobacco—if Mr. Martin goes . . . The children . . . Yearning for his presence.

December the 18th
At Home
Rusk County Texas

My own dear love,

I have just rec'd two letters from you. They were the first that I had got for over two weeks. The letters were written on the [illegible dates] & the fourth of this one that you wrote on the 1st has not come to hand yet but I presume I will get it before many days. This leaves us all well except myself. I have the measles but am getting along pretty well. I have been the worst case yet been sick twelve days have not eat as much in that length of time as I would hold in my hand but I think that with care I am now out of danger. I wanted to see you bad enough before I was taken sick & since I have been sick I have taken several big cries. It appeared to me that if I could only see my own dearly beloved husband I would get well. Ma come down & stayed four or five days & Pa come to see me too. Left yesterday. I am going up there next Tuesday if it is a pretty day. We are having some cold weather now big white frosts every morning. I fear that you will all suffer very much from sickness as you are so badly situated. I would have written to you before now if I had not been sick for you may rest assured that I will write weekly to you for next to reading your precious letters it is my greatest pleasure to write to my own loved companion who I know is as true & a husband as ever any woman was blessed with for you are most assuredly one of the greatest blessings of my life & I know that when you return home you would meet with as loving reception as anyone in the world could. I frequently anticipate that happy hour when I can as of old sit on your knee and be nestled in your arms. I sometimes dream that you are with us & I [think] that I am the happiest creature on earth but alas it is only a dream. I think that I will bake you a cake & send it by Mr. Martin if he goes. It is almost impossible to get any flour here now. I had some pretty wheat but it is young yet. I reserved it have had an extra good fence put up around it to secure it. If I can get some flour, I will make a cake for you and send it by some of the men that are coming back into camps. I have got you 5 lbs of pretty good tobacco & will send it the first opportunity. I now intend to send it by Mr. Miller or Henry one. I have a pair of pants & a pair of socks for you. Henry has promised to take your rubber coat & probably more. I could not make your blanket as my wool is not carded yet but you shall have it before next winter if it should be your misfortune as well as that of your family for you to be out that long. But I do hope that before that time rolls around you may all be at home with your families for be assured whenever it turns cold you are on my mind more than any other for when you are at home I could stand cold the best of the two for a little while but I know that you are now undergoing more than I can conceive or think of. Sometimes I think about it. It appears that it is more than I can stand but upon second thought there is no way to help it & it is my frequent prayer that you may have strength to go through it all safely & in the end of the struggle you may be permitted to return to the bosom of your family & once more enjoy that only blessedness which survived the fall for I know that no man in the service has a wife that thinks any more of than you do of yours nor is there a husband as father whose family can be any more devoted to them than your little group is to you. You are our nightly topic of conversation. They frequently wonder if Pa has seen the Yankees yet & if you have killed them. Jane don't like to talk about shooting since she has found out that they can shoot too she says that she expects that they are going to shoot her Pa because he left his gun here & can't shoot them. Arch is as mischievous as ever. He has fine fun catching chickens & putting them up in pens preparatory to moving. John went to his Granpa's day before yesterday for the first time in his life without us to stay all night. He is a good boy. Mary is now asleep beside me in the cradle. She is as funny as ever has some new shoes. It is the proudest thing that you ever saw in your life. She will soon be as large as Jane is as she has grown faster than any of our children ever did. I do wish you could see her now my dear husband. I intend to write to you weekly & if you do not get the letters it will not be my fault & you must do the same & let what come that you will know that you have a wife at home whose love will stand as unchanged as the forest oak for let us be . . . together you know that you have the most priceless gem that I possess.

Affectionately
N. F. Whatley

DECEMBER 25, 1862
WJW TO NFW

"You have now sold out. . . . You will not be near so lonely now. . . .
It is useless for one to say that I would like to be with you today."

*Winter at Arkansas Post . . . No shelter yet, delayed by tool shortage . . . Will
rifle pits defend against Union gunboats? . . . WJW has never seen a gunboat . . . Worried about the mail . . . Wants tobacco and letters . . . Put the boys
in school . . . Christmas gift! . . . Rumors of remounting.*

Arkansas Post Arkansas
December 25th 1862

Dear Wife,

One week has now rolled around since I have wrote to you, and as
it is my regular time to write, and having an opportunity to send it
I have concluded to do so, not that I have anything of importance to
write, but merely to let you know where I am and how I am getting
along. My health is as good as usual and apetite splendid. Christmas
is now on us and we are not yet in our houses and I fear it will be
sometime ere we get into them, for we have but few tools to work
with and they are indifferent but reckon we will get to enjoy some
of our labor before we have to leave, but some of the boys have been
expecting gun boats up as the river has rose about sixteen feet, but is
now falling again. It has been reported here that there were several
seen down about the mouth of the river, but I put no confidence
in it. We are still going ahead working on the rifle pits and getting
them ready to receive them when they come. A good many think
here that we will not be able to stand our hand with them when they
come. For my part I do not know, having never seen a gun boat of
any size, I am unable to tell what they can do, and this the first fort
I ever saw and don't know whether it is a good one or not, but it is
well covered with rail road iron and several large guns mounted in-

side besides several others on the outside, and it seems to me that it will be a hard matter for them to damage it much, without they can shoot into the port holes, which will take center shooting. General Churchill (who is now our commander) had us all out on general review last Saturday about two miles from here on the prairie. We made quite a grand display. When we are out on review we have to be regularly armed and equipped, with our guns, cartridge boxes, haversacks, canteens, and knapsacks. If you could see us you would say we were regular in the harness. We also have to go out in the same manner every Sunday morning where our equipage is all inspected, and everything required to be in good order. They are now getting us under pretty good control and have but little trouble with us. It has been now over a week since I have had a letter from you, and fear it will be some time before I do, as our mail, I understand is lying at Little Rock. Our Col [colonel] made arrangements to have it sent down to [Red Fork] about seven miles from here, but it has not been sent. Our courier is now gone to that place with our mail but I have no idea he will get us any letters. I fear that the mail will be very irregular here this winter, unless we send a courier direct to Little Rock for it, and even then we will not be able to get but one mail a week as it will take six days to make a trip and if it should rain much it will take longer than that. Mr. King got in last night from Texas. He stayed all night with your Pa. As he came up he informed that your Pa gave him a letter and some tobacco to bring to me but unfortunately someone stole them out of his saddlebags as he came on, somewhere that he stayed all night. I was very sorry for there are no two articles I prize so highly as tobacco and letters from home. I reckon it was written in relation to my business, and if so I have written and gave you and him full instructions about it which was to do as you thought best for situated as I am, it is impossible for me to know what is best for you to do, unless I was acquainted with the circumstances surrounding you. You have now sold out and perhaps will be moved before this reaches you. I want you to put both the little boys to school and keep them going steady and try and advance them all you can. You will not be near so lonely now, for I know your Ma will let Jane spend some time with you now that you will be so close that she can stay with you and carry on business almost as well as if she is at home. It is useless for one to say that I would like to be with you today, for I have not got language to express the joy and happiness I would enjoy if I was permitted to be with you. You will doubtless have a Christmas dinner or be at one somewhere else. I wish you much happiness, and hope you will enjoy yourself the best you can and not let my absence mar your happiness any more than you can help. We are going to have dinner at Christmas which if it is not so palatable or nice, will satisfy our appetite, and we will feel as well after we eat it as if we had been at a feast. I will be on duty today, and consequently will have no holiday, quite different from any Christmas I have ever spent, but we have no rest day here. Sunday is generally the big day. While I am writing about Christmas I will say Christmas gift and thereby take the advantage of you. If I could find anything here to buy I would send you and the children something for a Christmas present, but there is nothing in this country and if there were I have neither time nor opportunity to go out after it. We are not permitted to go out of camp at all without a pass and then not longer than twenty-four hours. I never leave the regiment unless sent out on a detail of some kind. I expect to send this by Hiram May who speaks of starting home today from Col Gillespie's Regiment and will make the trip in about ten days. Our boys are getting along tolerable well. I don't believe there is quite as much sickness here as there was ten days ago. I assisted last Sunday to bury a soldier [according to Masonic rites]. He was a member of Hancock's company and lived in Nacogdoches. We have sent up a petition for authority to hold a lodge of Masons in our regiment, and think we will succeed, which will have a good influence here in camp. My mess are all up now but Galloway and he is improving fast. Patrick is gone out to have a Christmas frolic. Dick and Colley are in fine health, both want to see some of the Texas girls very much. Colley is getting quite anxious to hear from home, has written several letters to his friends and has not received a line from any of them. There is some talk of remounting this regiment when six months run out from the time we were dismounted, and some say we will reorganize the 1st of March, but do not put much confidence in what I hear these days. I learn that there are a great many negroes in our country and fear if you have to hire out you will not be able to get much. King said there had been some ammunition taken from you. I gave old man Strange all the powder I had when I was at home last summer. Remember me to my friends, and give my love to my little children. I hope they will not forget me. I want you to write soon to your absent

Husband, who loves you.
W. J. Whatley

"This war will close in our favor and we will get to be a
full and independent people. . . . I somehow believe we will
meet again at the close of the war, if not before."

Doesn't know she's been ill, December 18 letter has not arrived . . . Hut building and tools scarcity . . . Arkansas Post miasma continues to kill Rusk County men . . . A lot about the future and Limestone County and wants Dr. Watkins to invest their capital in livestock . . . Capture of a Union boat loaded with provisions . . . Reflections on Lincoln's congressional message on compensated emancipation—slaves are property . . . Fredericksburg . . . Deserters . . . Illnesses and deaths of Rusk County men.

Arkansas Post, December 31st 1862

My Dear wife,

I again seat myself to write to you. The pleasantest task I have to perform. I wrote to you on the 25th and received a letter from you two days since, dated the sixth of this month. Was glad to hear from you, and to know that you were all well and getting along as well as

I could expect. I am suffering somewhat for the last three days with a pain in my side and breast, but I hope it is nothing serious, as I am able to be up all the time. I think I over done myself working on our houses with which we are progressing slowly on account of the scarcity of tools. We have ours completed however, and moved into it last night, and find it much more comfortable than being out of doors. The health here has not improved much. John Colley has been quite sick for two or three days but he is now improving and I hope he will soon be able to return to camps. Smith has been quite sick but he has nearly recovered. Lieut Evans had a discharge from the service and will start home tomorrow. I will send this letter by him, which will be a much better chance than by mail as our mails are getting to be very irregular of late though the last letter your Pa wrote me by hand was lost or stolen on the way, which I regretted very much, as their may have been some items of business in it that he desired me to respond to, but I presume I have written plainly enough about my affairs heretofore for him to understand me in full. You said in one of your letters that you wanted to settle in a stock country when we settle again. Your actions accord very well with mine. I have been in the notion of some time. I think we can get along a great deal easier and live much better if we were well settled in a good stock country [Limestone County, east of Waco] and if it is Gods will that I should live to return to you again I hope I will be prepared to appreciate peace and happiness, and try to make a good living and enjoy it. And I think if we had any ready money on hand it would be a good idea to lay it out in stock if they can be taken care of but I know you have none, for I don't want you to stint yourself or run out of money. You must keep enough on hand to answer your domestic purposes, but if you should get what is owing us I want your Pa to take it and invest in stock of some kind, so as it will be making something, as I don't think it will do to keep confederate money lying idle. It may be that he can use the notes to an advantage and if so it would probably be a good idea. I want him to take hold of my business and do just what he thinks is best and I will be satisfied. I would rather have almost any kind of property than Confederate money. So if he can't make a trade for stock he might lay out in land if he can get the money or use the notes. I received a letter the same day of yours from Uncle Jas. L. Burney. He lives in Limestone County. He is well settled and says he is doing well. Sends his love to you and children, and gives a pressing invitation to visit him at the close of the war. He is one of my very best uncles and one that I would like very much to see. His son William has gone home on a sick furlough or discharge. Poor fellow, he is unable to stand the service. Captain Nutt of Louisiana and his company a few days since captured a Yankee tow boat in the Mississippi River near the mouth of this river, and brought her up day before yesterday to this place.[1] She is heavily loaded with salt, flour, Irish potatoes, & [Ross] guns and ammunition and a quantity of other small article. She also had on her a very heavy mail and they all got a news paper to read, and some few love letters. I will send you a paper if I can get Evans to take it. We were very glad to see her come up for we had been without salt for three or four days and I reckon we would have been several days longer for there is none in Little Rock. They were going down to Vicksburg for supplies where they say they have a large force collecting, and tomorrow they say they are to make the attack upon Vicksburg. [The mid part of the letter is damaged. The following 15 lines are reconstructed] I read Lincoln's message [Second Message to Congress] yesterday.[2] He is strongly in favor of emancipation by compensation, thinks he could buy the freedom of negroes with less money than it will take to carry on the war, and estimates their expenses up to the first of July next. If the war should last that long at eleven hundred million of dollars, he seems to think that if we were compensated for our slaves and if the people would give them up and the old union could be reconstructed and thinks now that slaves are property and that the people of the North are as much responsible for them as we of the South, a notorious fact and one that they were not willing to acknowledge until now.[3] I think he is getting as tired of the war as we dare to be. We have the full account of the Fredericksburg fight from their own papers which gives us a complete victory. I have not been able to get hold of a paper as I want to send it to you. There are but few here that contain it and those who have them are unwilling to . . . General review and inspection today. I shall not go out because I don't feel like taking . . . began to look for our old friends, and I believe the boys will rejoice to see the day that the . . . it is said misery delights in company and I believe it is true, for we think they have as much [misery] as any of us. It seems now that everyone is keeping out of the war that can and a great many who are in it would get out . . . if they could. There seems to be a want of patriotism among us and the country is running wild with [deserters] and if we are ever whipped that thing will do it. I hope to survive the war and again return to the bosom of [my family]. I often ask God to spare the lives of my family and minister to your wants, both temporal and spiritual. I'm [thankful] that we are as well off as we are and I do believe that this war will close in our favor and we will get to be a full and independent people. I am unable to tell what we will do here or how long we will stay here, the sick are all ordered from the hospital to Pine Bluff that will not be able for duty in twenty days. Some say we are going to fight but I don't look for any fighting here soon at least until after the battle of Vicksburg which from all indications will not be a great while. I heard a day or two lines from Waterhouse's regiment. They are still suffering with sickness and a good many of the boys are dead among them are Wm Whitfield, Errel Thomas, Ed Parker, Bud McCall, and others that I don't now recollect. But I reckon you have heard the most of their deaths before now. It really seems that the southern portion of Rusk County has suffered more than any portions of country I can hear from. I want you to take care of yourself and children for I want to see you in a lively and healthy condition when I return home for I somehow believe we will meet again at the close of the war, if not before. Although I know that I am surrounded by disease and death is abroad in our land which is a debt we all have to pay sooner or later whether prepared or unprepared. We have just returned from inspections, it being the regular day to call the roll and note absentees. All who are able to go out have to go and answer to their names and all who are absent without leave have to be reported as deserters. This is done once in two months. Enclosed you will find two letters which I thought probably you would like to read. [Probably from his father in Alabama.] You can read them to the children and tell them who wrote them. I would love to see the dear little creatures and have them around me as in the days of yore. I can imagine now sometimes that I can see them in their infantile amusements. I will never forget their faces, write to me as before. I am always glad to hear from you. Give my love to all relations and friends. I will write to you as often as I can. I am as ever

> Your affectionate husband,
> WJ Whatley

1. Probably the *Blue Wing*. Its capture embarrassed the Union command and may have been the spur to General John A. McClernand to ignore Grant's order to concentrate on Vicksburg. On the Battle of Arkansas Post, see Sam Smith, "Stepping Stone to Vicksburg," *Civil War Trust*, accessed April 30, 2018, https://www.civilwar.org/learn/articles/battle-arkansas-post.

2. William E. Gienapp, ed., *This Fiery Trial: The Speeches and Writings of Abraham Lincoln* (New York: Oxford University Press, 2002), 143–50.

3. This is the sole instance in the correspondence that either Nancy or William refers to their enslaved as "slaves."

DECEMBER 31, 1862
A. H. WATKINS TO WJW

"Nancy is gone."

Texas Rusk co.   Mourvaul Tx Dec 31st 1862
Forward

Dear William

I recd yours of the 7th inst. And was truly glad to learn that you were still of the enjoyment of good health. Our family are also enjoying the same blessing, but I have sad news to communicate to you in relation to yours. Nancy is gone. She died on the 26 inst. At 2 O'clock PM of Typhoid Pneumonia supervening upon Measles. On the days I wrote to you last by Mr. King, I receive[d] intelligence from her that she was unwell and probably taking the measles which was so. Her mother went to see her immediately and remained with her until she recovered. We left her quite well on Wednesday and then sent Isham [his son] down to stay with her on Friday. She rode over to see Mr. Miller and at night was taken with chill followed by fever and considerable engorgement of the lungs. She sent immediately for Dr. Hubbard and for me, and I remained by her bed until she died. I also called in Doc Woolwin, hoping that something could be done to save her, though I believed from the first that she was bound to die. During the first day of her sickness her mind was clear. On the fourth she was somewhat flighty. On the 5th she was entirely wild, did not believe in the first part of her sickness that she was dangerously ill, and that we were alarmed unnecessarily, but I dreaded it as soon as I heard of her condition and found her much worse than I expected. She had all done for her that could be done, but it was of no avail. The disease progressed rapidly from day to day; until it closed her mortal existence in about 5 1/2 days. She died quiet and easy without a single struggle though entirely insensible and had been for two days. Oh how I desired that her reason might return and that I could talk to her and let her know that she was upon the verge of the spirit world but such was not the case. She is gone and while I am tonight writing in tears I fancy she is near the Throne and in the company of her dear brother [Jesse] who died just nine months before her. His body is on the bank of White River far from home here in Pine Grove. Their bodies are far apart, so with the immortal part. They are together and in the presence of the Lamb. Oh how hard it is to bear it but grace sustains me. I shall see them again, and we will live forever. Oh how I sympathize with you, but all I can do is to ask God in mercy to sustain you and grant you the blessing of seeing your children again. The shock to you will be heavy. Summon all your energy and ask for divine assistance to help you. He has only paid the debt that we must all soon pay. I will give you the particulars about the balance of your family. John, Jane, & Mary all have the measles. John is now in bed not fully broken out with them, but is doing well. Jane is up today. I dread her case on account of her cough but she has got along finely and has suffered no more than the balance of them. Mary is well. Hers was an easy case. Charley & Frank have also had them but they are both up. Burrel is taking them and will doubtless be down in a day or two more. Now the rest are all well except Manda. She has been confined. Her child is two days old (a girl). She is doing well and will doubtless be up in a few days. Your children are all here with us and have been for some days. They will be closely watched and cared for. As you doubtless know, they seem to be doubly dear to us. Since the death of their mother, the little girls are fast taking up with their Grandma and Jane, John, & Arch should be going to school, but I shall have to keep them at home on account of the measles for some time. Our school will be out in January the time so short that I will not send this session. If we get another I will send them both. I shall move everything you have up here. Nearly all of it is here and am now starting the wagon after the last of negroes and plunder. I have put Manda and her family in the kitchen I built at my Elliott place. I am building a house here for Marshal and his family. Birdwell will remain on our place and me on the other. I don't expect to hire [out] any of negroes. They would bring but little and perhaps might be badly clothed or taken care of. I shall put them all on the crop under except the women. They must make clothes for the balance, and try to make a support for all yours shall farm as mine does. If I fall a little short in meat, I can drive beeves from the farm next fall. You did not have enough corn. It took so much to fatten your hogs but I have a good supply and think I can get along without buying any. Stock hogs are very poor and will have to be fed a little all the time to keep them alive. Sows & pigs must be well fed. I shall bring all your hogs up here. They must be attended to. You have over thirty shoats that I have seen that will make meat hogs another year, and some from sows that have pigs. I may sell one or two of them as I shall be overstocked with pigs. Corn is now under $1.50 per bushel and but little to be had at any price. Your cattle had better remain where they are. They will do better there than here. I may probably bring up some of them that have young calves. I am at a loss to know what is best to do with your horses. It won't do to keep them here and feed them and have no use for them. I have sold Jesse's horse and he can use yours as a riding horse. The large mule I will need in the crop. The two young ones I have no use for. I have some thought of letting Jesse take them with him to the Prairie. The range is good thru this winter and he could take care of them. I believe I have detailed all my arrangements and plans to you as far as I can now recollect. Make any suggestions to me about any of your affairs you may desire. I have done for the best so far as I can now see. I am very much crowded with business at the present and doubtless have forgotten some things that I wanted to write but it must do so until I can have more time to think. I recd yesterday three letters from you and opened them. If I can get any chance at all I will send you the clothes you want. If you need anything write to me and if I can possibly send I will do so, or should you need money as your wages are but a trifle let me know it. Mr. Miller is at home and will not leave soon. His wife is nearly gone with consumption. She will not live long. We have had a warm, dry winter, very unfavorable to save pork. We are killing your hogs today. Our small grain looks well and is growing finely. You must write to me often. I will write again in ten days. By that time I think your family will be clear of the measles. Jane's health is greatly improved. I now have hopes that she will entirely regain her health. Jesse's health improved much while he was in Kaufman co [county] though he is still quite feeble and threatened with chronic diarrhea. He is now at home but will probably go back soon. I think it best to keep him traveling when he is able.

Yours truly,
A. H. Watkins

EPILOGUE

Despite the uncertainties of daily life during the Civil War, Nancy and William consistently sustained intense love and devotion. As reported in the last letter of the Whatleys' correspondence, William received the news of Nancy's death from Dr. Watkins on December 26, 1862.

> Nancy is gone . . . of Typhoid Pneumonia supervening upon Measles . . . sent immediately for Dr. Hubbard and for me, and I remained by her bed until she died . . . During the first day of her sickness her mind was clear. On the fourth she was somewhat flighty. On the 5th she was entirely wild. . . . She had all done for her that could be done, but it was of no avail. . . . She died quiet and easy without a single struggle though entirely insensible and had been for two days. . . . She is gone and while I am tonight writing in tears I fancy she is near the Throne and in the company of her dear brother [Jesse] who died just nine months before her.[1]

Drew Gilpin Faust documents the Civil War generation's fixation upon a "good death."[2] Families clung to the certainty that their loved ones who died serving in the armies experienced a dignified passing in communion with their savior. While the "good death" was reserved for men serving in the hostilities, Nancy Falkaday Whatley, as much as any soldier, was a Civil War casualty, and her death in the line of duty caring for her family was barely valued compared to a soldier's "good death."

William would serve in the Confederate army for the remainder of the war. After surrendering at Galveston with the wretched remnant of the Seventeenth, he returned to Rusk County in June of 1865 and died October 9, 1866, probably of tuberculosis, at the age of thirty-five. Before his death, he exchanged several emotional letters with his brother Seaborn in Alabama. Seaborn survived service with the Army of Northern Virginia; he was at the Battle of Fredericksburg and the Petersburg siege, and probably surrendered at Appomattox. Three letters written from Seaborn to William in 1866 survive, and in each it is clear that the Alabama Whatleys had urged William to move with his children there to live with childless Seaborn and their parents. The letters reflect an understanding of William's delicate health. Seaborn wrote movingly of his affection for William and his "little ones" and the Alabama family's warm desire for their relocation and joining their extended family.

With William's death, Dr. Watkins became the guardian for and benefactor of the orphaned children: John Strong, eleven; Archibald Henry, ten; Jane Burney, seven; and Nancy Lillie (Nannie), five.

According to Ruth Whatley Edmonson, her father, Archibald (1856–1918), my great-grandfather, did journey to Alabama to live with his uncle and his paternal grandparents. Seaborn Whatley provided a home for the family's numerous war orphans. The girls lived with their uncle and grandparents in their home, and the boys resided in a separate house where they basically raised themselves. Archibald matriculated at Cumberland University in Lebanon, Tennessee, was ordained a Cumberland Presbyterian minister, and served as a missionary to Mexico. He married an Indiana woman, Nancy Ann Barnett (1863–1927), and proved a controversial pastor in his last ministerial assignment at Carmichaels, Pennsylvania. Protesting the exclusion of black Presbyterian pastors from the local synod, he was expelled from his congregation. At age forty-two, he decided to enter medical school at Galveston, Texas, and in 1898, the newly minted doctor moved his family to southern Chihuahua, Mexico. Archibald became a physician for the international community of engineers and developers exploiting the mineral-rich resources of the states of Chihuahua and Durango. Predictably, he tired of that and moved quickly into ranching and dairying. Almost twenty years later, the family found itself caught in the crossfire of the Mexican Revolution. When Pancho Villa's revolt turned on the gringos in Chihuahua, the family took refuge in Texas. Archibald died at Rockdale, Texas, in 1918 while living with his sister, Jane Longmire. The Civil War and the Mexican Revolution framed his life.

His brother and sisters remained in East Texas. John (1855–1903) married Mary Adeline Longmire (1862–1903) and farmed near Kemp in Kaufman County. Jane (1860–1948) married another Longmire, Arthur (1854–1932), and they moved to Rockdale, Texas. Nancy Lillie (1861–1923) married Joab Melton (1856–1944), and they settled in Henderson County, one hundred miles from Caledonia. Archibald proved to be the only wanderer among his siblings.

Dr. Watkins died in 1881. His probated will read:

I give to Nancy F. Whatley, my eldest child, (now deceased) a full share of my estate the valuation thereof was fifteen hundred dollars but I hold the following which I intend for her children John S., Archibald H., Jane B., and Nancy L. Whatley the tract of land lying near Mt. Enterprise Rusk Co containing 240 acres which Wm J. Whatley sold to M. and Mrs. Hobson and I expended two hundred dollars of their money in recovering and perfecting the title to said land and I give them an additional one hundred acres out of my land my executrix to select the acres. I have expended for said children up to this time for board, clothing, and tuition about one hundred and fifty dollars each and propose that my executrix still continue them in school and make the same provisions for them as far as their raising and schooling is concerned as her own and if she find herself in a condition to do so that she gives to each one of them one horse saddle and bridle.

Today, one can still find the Pine Grove Church and Cemetery in Rusk County, which was established by Dr. Watkins in the 1840s. The church and cemetery are located off the Brachfield Road, an undulating, nondescript road off the Henderson bypass bordered by ranchettes until one turns onto a rural lane surrounded by the East Texas piney woods. A Texas Historical Commission plaque introduces a clearing framed by immature pine trees, new growth that has replaced cotton and agricultural land. Here, one finds an austere, whitewashed church built in the 1870s, a rustic pavilion for meetings and revivals, two corrugated privies, and a cemetery with a Dantesque warning at its gate:

KEEP GATE CLOSED

HOG PROBLEM

In the 1870s a new sanctuary replaced the original log structure from the 1840s. The church building is a gem of vernacular architecture—an understated, freshly painted pine-board structure. Its plainness, in and out, recalls a Shaker meeting room, and the old church affirms the intense, stern piety of the Cumberland Presbyterianism practiced by people like Nancy and William Whatley. The only tangible memories of Nancy Falkaday Whatley are these letters and her gravestone beside William's at Pine Grove. Her parents' graves are footsteps away.

NOTES

1. Archibald H. Watkins to WJW, December 31, 1862.

2. Drew Gilpin Faust, *This Republic of Suffering: Death and the American Civil War* (New York: Alfred A. Knopf, 2008), 3–31.

ACKNOWLEDGMENTS

The original impulse to publish my great-grandparents' letters was simply to get them in print for my children and grandchildren in order to connect them to their East Texas, Civil War ancestors. My father's family rarely reminisced about their past, so Nancy Falkaday Watkins Whatley and William Jefferson Whatley were barely names, and their East Texas and Rusk County another country for me. I had a dim awareness of what it was like for a woman during those years. As I uncovered Nancy Whatley's story, she emerged from the shadows and became a daily presence. Two generations ago, William's soldiering would have been the story with Nancy at his side, a silent appendage.

And most muted of all are the enslaved; it took another generation to tell some of their stories and resurrect the travails of enslaved Americans of the Lower South and Texas—and restore their identities. Along with connecting with my great-grandmother, I have had to confront our family's slaveholding past. Slavery in one's past is not unusual for a white American, but reading letter upon letter about the Whatleys' relationship with their slaves became personally transformative.

The Whatley letters entered my life sometime in the 1940s as I vaguely recall my aunts, my father's younger sisters, talking about them. In 1931, they—Ruth Whatley Edmonson and Anita Whatley Lorenz—contacted the Barker Center at the University of Texas at Austin. The center copied the originals by the photostatic process. Mrs. Edmonson retained the originals, and the Barker Center archived the photostats. After her death in 1982, the letters disappeared during the disposition of her estate.

I am particularly grateful to my daughter, Lisa Whatley, who in 1984 copied the photostats of the letters. Recently we closed the circle when she read the manuscript several times and applied her critical skills objectively and lovingly.

The Whatley letters have gotten this far due to the intervention of S. Kirk Walsh, a professional writer, accomplished in several genres. A terminally patient, forbearing person, Kirk has guided me through the publishing process, kept communications current with Louisiana State University Press, and supervised the editing and preparation of the manuscript. The nineteenth-century Whatleys would have appreciated her sterling qualities. Without Kirk, the Whatley letters would continue to languish in the Briscoe Center archives. She has given them life.

Longer ago than I will acknowledge, I transcribed the Whatley letters from those tired photostats of 1931 and ultimately prepared a primitive version of a manuscript, which I shared with Professor Jacqueline Jones, an eminent historian and chair of the History Department at the University of Texas. She encouraged me to keep at it and many times since then has directed me toward sources and research assistance. Her foreword to this book is excellence personified.

Dr. Jones connected me with her talented colleague Dr. Nick Roland, who guided my reading in the sources related to the Whatley letters. He patiently identified numerous misconceptions and errors—more than either of us would ever want anyone to count.

I owe a debt to the reader for the Louisiana State University Press, who critiqued and questioned my antique historiography and made valuable recommendations that led to months of personal reeducation in more contemporary research on Southern and Texas history, in particular about slavery and women. My generation acknowledged the evils of slavery without bothering to inquire about the realities of slave life in the antebellum Lower South. I treasure those months of reading and studying the work of the historians cited in the sources. I'm especially grateful to the following historians: Drew Gilpin Faust, who awakened in me an appreciation of the nuances in the lives of Civil War Southern women, which led to a fuller understanding of the uniqueness of my great-grandmother's experiences of 1862; Edward Baptist, who opened up the actual lives of slaves in the Lower South; Randolph Campbell, whose perceptions and data about slavery in Texas are an enduring contribution to a revised evaluation of Texas's dance of death with slavery; and Bertram Wyatt-Brown and James Oakes, who concretized the realities of Southern honor.

The late Mary Elizabeth Whatley Jones of Abilene, Texas, was a lifelong student of Whatley family genealogy and produced *The Whatley Grandfathers* and *Whatley Grandfathers Revised*, which I consulted to piece out the journeys of the Whatleys and Watkinses from Virginia and North Carolina to Rusk County, Texas. She was an excellent researcher and great lady.

I want to recognize my East Texas friends who have supported this project. Vicki Betts of the Muntz Library at the University of Texas at Tyler read the manuscript and returned it to me with a month's worth of revisions and corrections. She is an excellent historian and accomplished scholar with an encyclopedic knowledge of Civil War East Texas. John Dulin, a historian of Rusk County and genealogist extraordinaire, directed me to Whatley-Watkins family arcana. John Brooks of Rockdale, Texas, located my grandfather's grave and forwarded references to the Rockdale descendants of Nancy and William Whatley. Henderson genealogist Lynda Jones introduced my wife Melba and me to Rusk County and guided us to memorable Pine Grove Church and Cemetery, which I have since revisited.

My friend, writer, and master journalist Chris Tomlinson of the *Houston Chronicle* read and commented on an early version of the manuscript, which sent me back to the drawing board. Peggy Pickle unceasingly has reminded me that I needed to keep moving. Stretching tolerance for aging, John Worrall drove me on a journey to East Texas for another Pine Grove visit, a tour of Mansfield Battlefield, and to locate the crossroads of Caledonia. Laura Grady did a lot of scut work for me—cheerfully. And faithful friends Samantha Smoot and Marie Crane cheered me on, probably more than they realized.

Ellen Clarke Temple on several occasions gave me sound direction about the publishing process and was always encouraging.

The staff of the Briscoe Center for American History and its director, Dr. Don Carleton, have been unfailingly helpful during many visits there to examine the Whatley letters. They are valuable stewards of Texas history.

I thank the entire staff at Louisiana State University Press. In particular, Editor-in-Chief Rand Dotson took a risk with this project, and recognized the value to scholarship in the Whatley letters. Gratitude to Senior Editor Catherine L. Kadair for her expertise and attention as she ably oversaw and guided the production of this book from start to finish. Also, thanks to the entire marketing team of the press for its assistance in taking the book out into the larger world. And respect and appreciation for Michael Taber's index.

Finally, I've dedicated this book to my spouse, Melba Davis Whatley. Her constant interest in the project spurred me to continue in my efforts over the years—and publish Nancy Falkaday Whatley's memorable story.

SOURCES

Anderson, John Q., ed., *Brokenburn: The Journal of Kate Stone, 1861–1868.* Baton Rouge: Louisiana State University Press, 1955.

Bailey, Anne J. "The Texas Cavalry's Race to Reinforce Arkansas Post, January 1863." *East Texas Historical Journal* 28.1 (1990): 45–56. Available at http://scholarworks.sfasu.edu/ethj/vol28/iss1/9.

Baptist, Edward E. *The Half Has Never Been Told: Slavery and the Making of American Capitalism.* New York: Basic Books, 2014.

Beckert, Sven. *Empire of Cotton: A Global History.* New York: Knopf, 2014.

Berlin, Ira. *Many Thousands Gone: The First Two Centuries of Slavery in North America.* Cambridge, MA: Belknap Press of Harvard University Press, 1998.

Betts, Vicki. "'They Call It Patriotism': Homespun as Politics in the South, 1860–1861." 2002. Accessed April 30, 2018, http://apps.uttyler.edu/vbetts/homespun%20patriotism.htm.

Blight, David W. *Race and Reunion: The Civil War in American Memory.* Cambridge, MA: Belknap Press of Harvard University Press, 2001.

Boles, John B. *The Great Revival: Beginnings of the Bible Belt.* Lexington: University Press of Kentucky, 1996.

Boles, John B., and Evelyn Thomas Nolen, eds. *Interpreting Southern History: Historiographical Essays in Honor of Sanford W. Higginbotham.* Baton Rouge: Louisiana State University Press, 1987.

Bowman, Shearer Davis. *At the Precipice: Americans North and South during the Secession Crisis.* Chapel Hill: University of North Carolina Press, 2010.

Bridenbaugh, Carl. *Myths and Realities: Societies of the Colonial South.* Baton Rouge: Louisiana State University Press, 1952.

Brown, Norman D., ed. *Journey to Pleasant Hill: The Civil War Letters of Captain Elijah P. Petty, Walker's Texas Division, CSA.* San Antonio: University of Texas, Institute of Texan Cultures, 1982.

Buenger, Walter L. *Secession and the Union in Texas*. Austin: University of Texas Press, 1984.

Burkhardt, George S. *Confederate Rage, Northern Wrath: No Quarter in the Civil War*. Carbondale: Southern Illinois University Press, 2007.

Burton, Orville Vernon. *In My Father's House Are Many Mansions: Family and Community in Edgefield, South Carolina*. Chapel Hill: University of North Carolina Press, 1985.

Bynum, Victoria E. *The Long Shadow of the Civil War: Southern Dissent and Its Legacies*. Chapel Hill: University of North Carolina Press, 2010.

———. *Unruly Women: The Politics of Social and Sexual Control in the Old South*. Chapel Hill: University of North Carolina Press, 1992.

Campbell, Randolph B. *An Empire for Slavery: The Peculiar Institution in Texas, 1821–1865*. Baton Rouge: Louisiana State University Press, 1989.

———. "Fighting for the Confederacy: The White Male Population of Harrison County in the Civil War." *Southwestern Historical Quarterly* 104.1 (July 2000).

———. *Gone to Texas: The Lone Star State*. 2nd ed. New York: Oxford University Press, 2012.

Carrigan, William D. *The Making of a Lynching Culture: Violence and Vigilantism in Central Texas*. Urbana: University of Illinois Press, 2006.

Cash, W. J. *The Mind of the South*. New York: Alfred A. Knopf, 1941.

Clinton, Catherine. *Stepdaughters of History: Southern Women and the American Civil War*. Baton Rouge: Louisiana State University Press, 2016.

Cobb, James C. *Away down South: A History of Southern Identity*. New York: Oxford University Press, 2005.

Cutrer, Thomas W. *Ben McCulloch and the Frontier Military Tradition*. Chapel Hill: University of North Carolina Press, 1993.

Davis, David Brion. *The Problem of Slavery in the Age of Revolution, 1770–1823*. Ithaca: Cornell University Press, 1975.

Faust, Drew Gilpin. *Mothers of Invention: Women of the Slaveholding South in the American Civil War*. Chapel Hill: University of North Carolina Press, 1996.

———. *This Republic of Suffering: Death and the American Civil War*. New York: Alfred A. Knopf, 2008.

Fischer, David Hackett. *Albion's Seed: Four British Folkways in America*. New York: Oxford University Press, 1989.

Ford, Lacy K. *Deliver Us from Evil: The Slavery Question in the Old South*. New York: Oxford University Press, 2009.

Gallaway, B. P. *The Ragged Rebel: A Common Soldier in W. H. Parsons' Texas Cavalry, 1861–1865*. Austin: University of Texas Press, 1988.

——, ed. *Texas, The Dark Corner of the Confederacy: Contemporary Accounts of the Lone Star State in the Civil War*. Lincoln: University of Nebraska Press, 1994.

Gienapp, William E., ed. *This Fiery Trial: The Speeches and Writings of Abraham Lincoln*. New York: Oxford University Press, 2002.

Glasrud, Bruce A., and James M. Smallwood, eds. *The African American Experience in Texas*. Lubbock: Texas Tech University Press, 2007.

Grear, Charles D., ed. *The Fate of Texas: The Civil War and the Lone Star State*. Fayetteville: University of Arkansas Press, 2008.

——. *Why Texans Fought in the Civil War*. College Station: Texas A&M University Press, 2010.

Herman, Arthur. *How the Scots Invented the Modern World*. New York: Random House, 2001.

Howell, Kenneth W., ed. *The Seventh Star of the Confederacy: Texas during the Civil War*. Denton: University of North Texas Press, 2009.

Johnson, Walter. *River of Dark Dreams: Slavery and Empire in the Cotton Kingdom*. Cambridge, MA: Belknap Press of Harvard University Press, 2017.

Jones, Mary Elizabeth Whatley. *Whatley Grandfathers Revised (The Ornan Whatley Line): Including Biographies of Heard and Crook Ancestors*. Abilene, TX: self-pub., 1990. Original ed. 1973.

Klarman, Michael J. *The Framers' Coup: The Making of the United States Constitution*. New York: Oxford University Press, 2016.

Liles, Deborah M., and Angela Boswell, eds. *Women in Civil War Texas: Diversity and Dissidence in the Trans-Mississippi*. Denton: University of North Texas Press, 2016.

Litwack, Leon F. *Been in the Storm So Long: The Aftermath of Slavery*. New York: Alfred A. Knopf, 1979.

Loyd, Doyal T. "Morgan H. Looney and His Gilmer School, 1861–1871." *East Texas Historical Journal* 15.1 (1970): 20–23. Available at http://scholarworks.sfasu.edu/ethj/vol15/iss1/7.

Mahoney, Timothy R. *From Hometown to Battlefield in the Civil War Era: Middle Class Life in Midwest America*. New York: Cambridge University Press, 2016.

Marten, James. *The Children's Civil War*. Chapel Hill: University of North Carolina Press, 2000.

McCurry, Stephanie. *Confederate Reckoning: Power and Politics in the Civil War South*. Cambridge, MA: Harvard University Press, 2010.

McPherson, James M. *Battle Cry of Freedom: The Civil War Era*. New York: Oxford University Press, 1988.

———. *For Cause and Comrades: Why Men Fought in the Civil War*. New York: Oxford University Press, 1997.

Mohr, Clarence L. *On the Threshold of Freedom: Masters and Slaves in Civil War Georgia*. 1986; Baton Rouge: Louisiana University Press, 2001.

Morgan, Edmund S. *American Slavery, American Freedom: The Ordeal of Colonial Virginia*. New York: W. W. Norton, 1975.

Noe, Kenneth W. *Reluctant Rebels: The Confederates Who Joined the Army after 1861*. Chapel Hill: University of North Carolina Press, 2010.

Oakes, James. *Freedom National: The Destruction of Slavery in the United States, 1861–1865*. New York: W. W. Norton, 2013.

———. *The Ruling Race: A History of American Slaveholders*. New York: W. W. Norton, 1998.

———. *Slavery and Freedom: An Interpretation of the Old South*. New York: Knopf, 1990.

Rable, George C. *Civil Wars: Women and the Crisis of Southern Nationalism*, Urbana: University of Illinois Press, 1991.

Reynolds, Donald E. *Texas Terror: The Slave Insurrection Panic of 1860 and the Secession of the Lower South*. Baton Rouge: Louisiana State University Press, 2007.

Rothman, Adam. *Slave Country: American Expansionism and the Origins of the Deep South*. Cambridge, MA: Harvard University Press, 2005.

Schroeder-Lein, Glenna R. *The Encyclopedia of Civil War Medicine*. Armonk, NY: M. E. Sharpe, 2008.

Sellers, Charles. *The Market Revolution: Jacksonian America, 1815–1846*. New York: Oxford University Press, 1991.

Sheehan-Dean, Aaron. *Why Confederates Fought: Family and Nation in Civil War Virginia*. Chapel Hill: University of North Carolina Press, 2009.

Smith, Sam. "Stepping Stone to Vicksburg." *Civil War Trust*, accessed April 30, 2018, https://www.civilwar.org/learn/articles/battle-arkansas-post.

Torget, Andrew J. *Seeds of Empire: Cotton, Slavery, and the Transformation of the Texas Borderlands, 1800–1850*. Chapel Hill: University of North Carolina Press, 2015.

Winfrey, Dorman H. *A History of Rusk County, Texas*. Waco: Texian Press, 1961.

Wohlleben, Peter. *The Hidden Life of Trees*. Trans. Jane Billinghurst. Vancouver: Greystone Books, 2015.

Woodward, C. Vann, ed. *Mary Chesnut's Civil War*. New Haven: Yale University Press, 1981.

Wyatt-Brown, Bertram. *Honor and Violence in the Old South*. New York: Oxford University Press, 1986.

———. *Southern Honor: Ethics and Behavior in the Old South*. New York: Oxford University Press, 2007.

INDEX

Civil War battles and skirmishes:
Antietam, 41, 79n1, 107, 107n1; Fort
Hindman, xxxvii, xliii(n52); Freder-
icksburg, 123, 130; Helena, 63; Hills
Plantation, 24–25; in Kentucky, 67,
69n1; Manassas, 41; Mansfield,
xxxviii, xxxix, 40n2; Milliken's Bend,
xxx–xxxi; Pea Ridge, xxxvi, xlii(n48);
Prairie Grove, 112; Sabine Pass, xxxi;
Vicksburg, 102, 113, 124; William on,
1, 13, 21–22, 24–25, 48–49, 58, 63, 67,
99, 106–7, 112–13, 123
Clarendon, AR, 47, 49n1, 51, 76
Clinton, John, 2
Clinton, William, 2
clothing, 51–52, 65, 76, 81; sending to
William of, 42, 61, 86, 96, 106, 116–17,
128; shortages of, 81
Colby (landowner), 39, 42, 74
Colley, John, 22, 61, 68, 98, 99; health
of, 59, 120, 122; relaying of letters by,
64, 65, 78
Coltharp, T. S., 53
Confederacy: and conscription, xxxiii,
xxxiv, 2, 5, 19, 31, 37, 63, 69, 77, 86;
embargo on Northern clothing goods,
67, 69n2; mail delivery by, xxxi;
Northern blockade of, xxxi–xxxii;
rumors about British and French
recognition of, xxxvi, 81, 84n1; Rusk
County volunteers for, xxvi; Whatleys' commitment to, xviii, xxxiii–
xxxiv, 55, 82, 108, 124
Confederate Army: cavalry in, xxxiv–
xxxv, 4, 6n2, 25; discipline in, 39,
68; drills and reviews in, 38, 68, 82,
101, 119; duties in, xvii, 48, 57, 82;
enlistment bounties in, xxxiii, 41,
43n1; furloughs in, 38, 106; soldiers'
pay in, 13, 14n3, 41–42, 66, 110, 114;
Texas regiments in, 63, 67, 120–21;
Trans-Mississippi Department of,

xxxv, xxxvi. *See also* Civil War battles
and skirmishes; Seventeenth Texas
Cavalry
Confederate money, xviii, xxxii, 4, 91, 122
Confederate News, 67, 86
Confiscation Acts, xxx
Conscription Act of 1862, xxxiii, xxxiv,
19; exemptions from, 86; and substitutes, 5; William on, 2, 31, 37, 63,
69, 77
Corinth, MS, 4, 6n1, 58, 59n2
Cornel, John, 32
cotton: embargo of, xxxi, 6n3; ginning
of, xxxii, xxxviii, 5, 6n3, 8, 11, 16, 34,
44; monoculture in, xxiii; and Northern blockade, xxxi–xxxii; shortage
of cards, xxxi, xxxviii, 69n2, 73, 81,
91, 95–96
Crump, R. P., 2
Culberson, Colonel, 69
Cumberland Presbyterian Church, xxiii,
xxxiv, xl(n6)
Curtis, Samuel Ryan, Gen., xxxvi,
xlii(n47), 24, 48–49

Davis, Captain, 8
Davis, Jefferson, xxvii, 114
Davis, Mr., 69–70
deserters, xviii, 124
DeValls Bluff, 22, 27
disease, xviii–xix; among troops, 4,
40n1, 41, 54n1, 57, 77, 80, 91, 104, 108,
112, 124; black tongue, 8; brain fever,
80; fever, 15, 16, 43, 44, 60, 70; pneumonia, 77, 98, 125. *See also* measles
drought, xviii, xxvi, xxxviii; Nancy on,
16, 18, 27, 46, 70, 71
drunkenness, 94

Easley, Jack, 4, 25
Elliott, Ed, 105, 114
Elliott, John and Louis, 16